THE COLOR
OF LOVE

THE COLOR OF LOVE

A STORY OF A MIXED-RACE JEWISH GIRL

MARRA B. GAD

BOLDEN

AN **AGATE** IMPRINT

CHICAGO

First printing November 2019

Printed in the United States of America

10 9 8 7 6 5 4 3 2 1   19 20 21 22 23

Library of Congress Cataloging-in-Publication Data

Names: Gad, Marra B., 1970- author.
Title: The color of love : a story of a mixed-race Jewish girl / by Marra B. Gad.
Description: Chicago : Bolden , an Agate imprint, [2019] | "A memoir about a mixed-raced Jewish woman who chooses to help her estranged Great-Aunt Nette after she develops Alzheimer's, a disease that erases Nette's prejudices, allowing Marra to develop a relationship with the woman who shunned her in youth"--Provided by publisher.
Identifiers: LCCN 2019010449 (print) | LCCN 2019012018 (ebook) | ISBN 9781572848344 (ebook) | ISBN 1572848340 (ebook) | ISBN 9781572842755 (pbk. : alk. paper) | ISBN 157284275X (pbk. : alk. paper)
Subjects: LCSH: Gad, Marra B., 1970- | Racially mixed women--United States--Biography. | Racially mixed women--Race identity--United States--Biography. | African American women--Biography. | Jewish women--United States--Biography. | Jewish families--United States--Biography.
Classification: LCC E184.A1 (ebook) | LCC E184.A1 G123 2019 (print) | DDC 306.85/089924--dc23
LC record available at https://lccn.loc.gov/2019010449

Cover design by Morgan Krehbiel
Author photo by Bobby Quillard
Cover artwork elements © WeWorkForThem www.youworkforthem.com

Bolden Books is an imprint of Agate Publishing. Agate books are available in bulk at discount prices. For more information, visit agatepublishing.com.

For my mother, Ellie, who always wants me to
sing so that people can hear me . . .
including this song of myself

Prologue

My friend Rosa often says she is amazed that I can be loving. Or kind. Or happy. She says that because she knows a fair bit about what some like to call my "complicated" existence. And I'd like to think I am all of those things.

"How do you not hate everyone?" she frequently asks after I share a story.

"Because I'm the luckiest girl on earth," I say. "Look at my life!"

I have incredible, supportive, loving parents. A brother and a sister, each of whom I get to connect with in ways that are authentic and meaningful, even when we want to kill each other. As siblings sometimes do. I have two nieces and a nephew, who could not be more delicious. Wonderful, kind, hilarious, ride-or-die friends. Great skin. An incredible career producing film and television, working with some of the very best in the business. And I have a lens into the world that very few share.

I am the luckiest.

I was born in April 1970 to a young, unmarried, white Jewish girl from Manhattan. When she learned that she was pregnant, she went to her rabbi for help, telling him that she could not keep the baby and that her parents would certainly kill her if her pregnancy were to be found out. And so, as he had done many times before with other girls in her condition, he sent her away from the city—upstate to Binghamton—so that she could keep her pregnancy hidden.

A few years prior, my beloved late cousin Adrienne Mae and her husband, Hal, had connected with this same rabbi, despite the fact that they lived in Milwaukee and he was in New York. My cousins were infertile, and this rabbi had made it his mission to make sure that Jewish babies in need of homes were placed with Jewish families. They adopted two children through him. Most rabbis have causes that are dear to them. And this cause was his.

Meanwhile, my parents had been trying to get pregnant for nearly a year before going to a doctor. According to the limited fertility testing available in 1969, my father had a low sperm count, and the doctor suggested my parents use artificial insemination so that the baby would be "half theirs."

My mother saw the horrified look on my father's face, and without missing a beat, she informed the doctor that they would be adopting. This way, she told him, the baby would be "all theirs."

My mother called Adrienne. Adrienne called the rabbi. And he called my parents, telling them he had a girl who was due in April and that they could have her baby.

Interestingly, they had arranged to adopt a baby prior to being offered me, but the birth mother changed her mind once her baby was born, leaving my parents devastated. It was not through the rabbi who eventually sorted us out, but through a more traditional agency. I thank God every day that this other woman changed her mind, for I believe with every fiber of my being that my parents didn't get the first baby because they were meant to get me.

Infertility is fairly common in the Jewish community. I've often joked that it's because we are inbred, but there is a touch of truth to that. Throughout history, the Jewish people have tended to keep to themselves, often living separately from other people in their geographic homes, with marriages being born within the community. Adoption has always been a solution to that issue, even in the 1960s and '70s, when there was still a fair bit of shame and secrecy around adopting. Couples would go to great lengths to get a child who looked like them so as to avoid questions.

Adrienne and Hal had that luxury. My parents did not.

I was born on my father's birthday. My parents were out celebrating and received a message that I had arrived and that they should head to New York to pick me up. And so they flew from Chicago to Binghamton and went straight to the hospital.

My mother tells me that my adult lifestyle and colorful—and, at times, dramatic—personality are not a surprise, given that I was kept in a private nursery surrounded by guards to ensure I did not end up in the wrong hands. When the attorney arrived to hand me off to my parents, he went into the nursery, leaned over to look into the crib, and turned in shock to the neonatal nurse. "Are you sure that's the right baby?"

"That's the baby," she replied.

I was the color of milk chocolate and had a head full of dark, curly hair. He apparently became even paler than usual, his face having drained of all color.

Today, there would be a bidding war for a baby who looked like me. But that was not the case in 1970. And while it seems my biological mother was a young, unwed, and—shall we say—passionate creature, she was also smart and forward-thinking enough to know it was unlikely she would find a family willing to knowingly take a mixed-race baby. And so she did not disclose that her lover had been black and left the rabbi, his attorney, and my parents to sort it all out.

The rabbi apologized to my parents and told them

they didn't have to take me. After all, a mixed-race baby wasn't what they had signed up for. But my parents and I had already fallen in love. Returning me was not an option because, to them, no mistake had been made. When they looked into my crib, they didn't see a mixed-race baby— they saw their new daughter. And, at three days old, I was taken home to Chicago.

Unlike most adoptions today, my adoption was closed. My parents never met my biological mother. My mother saw her through the window of her hospital room and has only ever said that she was a "bottle-blonde" young woman. The only thing we know about my biological father is that he was black. I'm not sure if he was ever told I exist. I've never been contacted by the biological relatives who might be out in the world, nor have I ever sought to find them. And while I had to be carried in another woman's womb, my family has always been the one I was meant to have. I chose them for a reason. And yes—I chose them and not the other way around.

My parents had always hoped to have a large family, so they told the rabbi almost immediately that they would like to be put back on the list for another baby. Any baby. But, as is known to happen with infertile couples who adopt, my mother became pregnant with my sister shortly after I arrived and then with my brother eight years after that.

My extended family's reaction to my arrival, much like me,

was mixed. It was one thing for my parents to have adopted, but it was quite another that I wasn't white. Within days, calls came in from both sides of the family for "paper proof" that I had actually been born a Jew. One relative suggested that a private detective be hired to find my biological parents so that there would be absolute surety about "what" I was. On my father's side of the family, the reaction was so negative that it created an irrevocable and very painful break in their relationship. One he felt compelled to make when it was clear I was not going to be accepted and loved without question. Again and again, my parents informed family and friends that I was simply their daughter, and that if that wasn't good enough, they didn't need to come to the house again. And our circle grew consistently smaller as a result.

It is the job of any parent to protect their child. But for my parents, this job was elevated to a state of constant defense none of us were wholly prepared for. To this day, I see my mother's physicality change when someone looks askance at us when she is introduced as my mother—or me as her daughter. She stands up as tall as she possibly can. She pushes her tiny shoulders back. And she sets her jaw in a way that always says to me that she is ready.

With my parents, there was never flight. There was only fight.

And given the waters we have had to navigate, as a family and as individuals, having parents prepared to—at times quite literally—take on the world is a gift for which I will never be able to express my gratitude.

Like I said: I am the luckiest girl in the world.

Growing up in the 1970s and '80s, I never saw myself in anyone around me. Not at school. Not at synagogue. Not at camp. Not on television. Not in magazines. Today, I am starting to see myself reflected everywhere—more and more shades of life breathing in beautiful brown combinations, each of them a bit different and as unique as my own. I see a celebration of us and others as being beautiful, just as we are, that has been a long time coming.

The party, however, is still not in fullest swing.

In the Jewish community, there has always been some level of confusion around the nature of my brown existence— especially around the notion that I was born a Jew and that I did not convert to become one. Jews, many believe, are white. To some, I am simply unacceptable. The first time I heard the word *nigger*, it came from the mouth of a member of my own community.

To this day, I am routinely asked when I go to synagogue if I am "in the right place." I am assumed to be "the help"—the kitchen help, someone's nanny. Rarely am I simply welcomed with a smile like my Eastern European–looking family members. Last year, on Yom Kippur, the holiest day of the Jewish year, an usher chased me down the hall at a synagogue my brother's family was considering joining. "What are you doing here?" she demanded.

"I'm here to pray," I replied. "What are you doing here?"

In the black community, the struggles for some to make sense of me are similar. On this side, the widely held belief is that black people are Christian or Muslim but not Jewish. When I was working as a musical theater actress and cast in an all-black play, I stood in the hallway and heard the majority of the cast demand that the director recast me. "She's Jewish!" they said. "She's not really black."

When Marvel's *Black Panther* film came out—arguably one of the most seminal moments in film history because it was the first action-adventure film of its magnitude with an almost exclusively black cast—groups of my black friends organized to go see the film, wanting to not only support the critical business around it but also celebrate inclusion on the screen. When I noticed that I had not been invited to join any of those parties, I asked a friend why.

"You're just not that kind of black, Marra."

People often pressure me to choose which group I belong to, as if I can simply deny being part of the other or force my whole self into a single space. I've had people tell me I must self-identify as black because it is important and because, if my skin is brown, society will never let me be white. That I am half-white does not seem to matter. Some believe it should not matter. On the other hand, a rabbi once told me, "You don't have to be mixed race. You can just be Jewish. Maybe that would be easier." But being Jewish is a religion. The two, in my version of the story, should have nothing to do with each other.

Jews are white and black people aren't Jewish. And yet, here I am: a mixed-race, Jewish unicorn.

The idea that I can choose at all is almost comical. I cannot simply decide to be only one of the things I am. I cannot disregard, ignore, or marginalize the rest. I don't want to. And given the relative discomfort displayed by people in both communities, I don't see what the benefit would be. It would be like picking between two teams that can't fully see my beauty and aren't quite sure they want to claim me. And that's really no choice at all.

Of course, not everyone behaves this way or finds my background uncomfortable. There are kindred spirits everywhere. But even friends of many decades who fall quite neatly into one community or the other have told me I am "different" in the slightly uncomfortable way. Not in the complimentary way.

I have never understood why the unusual intersection where my race and religion exist matters at all, much less so much. And to so many. If it's so important that we are all one thing or the other, why is the woman who sent me to the kitchen with the catering staff—in the synagogue my grandfather helped pay for—the same woman who tans herself a shade well beyond my shade of brown? Why do black men who want to date women of faith choose "God-fearing Christian girls" but not me, a God-loving Jewish girl?

I have never understood why I am not simply seen as human, which is the way I see people. To me, being human—literally and figuratively—is, arguably, the greatest equalizer of them all. In the Torah/Old Testament, there is a phrase that has always summed it up for me: *B'tzelem Elohim*. It means "in the image of God," and it refers to all creation. That should be enough for any of us. For all of us to be able to see our individual designs as beautiful. And as godlike. But sadly, for some—really for most—it is not.

In my life, I have found there are truths many people do not want to hear. I have been told that the stories of my life could not or did not happen. No one wants to think racism and intolerance exist among people who know so well—too well—what it feels like to be discriminated against. Jews and black people certainly know. And should know better.

For many, identity is literally a black-and-white matter. For those of us who live in the gorgeous places in between, we must choose how to manage what comes when we are "othered" by . . . others.

This is the story of how I have come to know who I am when faced with exactly this, and I know the choice is mine.

And mine alone. It is *because* of everything I have ever experienced, and the fact that I exist in this unique form, that I am able to choose as I do. And not despite it.

And, for me, the choice is always love.

PART ONE

the wounds have changed me.
i am so soft with scars
my skin
breathes and beats stars.
—NAYYIRAH WAHEED

Chapter One

"YOU REALLY ARE VERY PRETTY." MY GREAT-AUNT Nette took a sip of her martini, surveying me up and down like a horse on the auction block, the jewels on her fingers catching the light. "No date?"

My sister Alisa's wedding was the first in our family. And when you are Jewish, getting married is an important, celebrated, and at times demanded thing. One of the most brilliant things about the classic 2002 film *My Big Fat Greek Wedding* is that the story line about the tremendous pressure to get married and have babies resonated, even if you were not Greek. The movie depicted an absolute truth for life as a Greek daughter, and in many ways, it is an absolute truth for Jewish girls too. My great-aunt Nette liked getting married so much that she did it five times. Interestingly, no one in our family was ever invited to any of the weddings.

The *ketubah*—the Jewish wedding contract—had just been signed, and Nette, with her multiple marriages behind her, was one of the people my sister had chosen for the honor. My sister was the perfect great-niece for Nette. She adored Alisa, and Alisa adored her. To me, Nette, at four feet, ten inches tall and exactly eighty-nine pounds, had always seemed enormous. She was constantly looking down.

"This really isn't the kind of baptism by fire that I would want for a date, Aunt Nette," I said. "A family wedding is a big thing."

I hoped this would send her away, and I breathed deep, inhaling the gorgeous perfume of the lilies that adorned the room. With about fifteen minutes left before the ceremony, the families and the bridal party had gathered to prepare for the processional. I was about to sing as Alisa and Keith walked down the aisle. I stood off in a corner, warming up my voice and silently praying I would not begin to weep when I saw my sister.

Before Nette approached, I had been, as my vocal coach had taught me, breathing in and out and running scales to warm up. Even on good day, my voice often wavered a bit on the high notes. When I knew my performance needed to be extra special, I was always concerned about it.

"If you're a lesbian, we would be fine with that," Nette said, looking me coldly in the eye. "It would probably help everyone to understand why you're not married"—I took another deep, coach-approved breath—"at your age."

"I'm *not* a lesbian. I just didn't choose to bring a date," I said. "Now if you'll excuse me . . ."

I am fortunate that this pressure to marry has never come from my mother. Her desire is for each of her children to be happy, and she has always clearly understood that happiness takes a different path for every person. "If happiness means getting married because you love someone, then by all means, get married," she has said. "Marriage isn't for everyone, and it's not for everyone at the same time. Just be happy. Everything else will work itself out."

My sister and my brother both met their spouses and married when they were in their early twenties. Even without the internal familial messaging about marriage, my sister set her course when she was a teenager. When Alisa was fifteen, she spent the summer at our camp in Wisconsin, babysitting for our rabbi's two youngest children. As she was packing, she smiled and said, "Marra, I'm going to get a boyfriend this summer."

And, ever the patronizing older sister, I smiled back and said, "Of course you will."

It turns out that my sister is an amazing manifestor, and she did get a boyfriend that summer. My family went up to camp to visit for the day, and there he was: an eighteen-year-old waterfront staffer named Keith. As we were quite close in age, I already knew him. Although we had different sets of friends, we had been at camp at the same time, and camp is a small place. That said, like many other people, Keith did not realize that Alisa and I were sisters. We look nothing alike, and our personalities are as different as are our looks.

When we arrived to be introduced to "the Boyfriend," as we had taken to calling him, Keith stopped in his tracks. "She is your sister?"

Almost at the same time, I exclaimed, "He is your boyfriend?"

A sitcom writer could not have written it better.

But there he was. Utterly smitten with my little sister. And from that summer on, he and Alisa were completely devoted to each other. There was never a "break" like the one Ross and Rachel took on *Friends*—they even dated long distance when my sister went to the University of Iowa. When I realized after about two years that Keith wasn't going anywhere, I sat my sister down and tried to talk to her about the importance of, well, playing the field a bit.

"I think boys are like ice cream," I began. "How do you know that butter pecan is your favorite flavor if you've never tried mint chocolate chip?"

Without missing a beat, Alisa looked at me and replied, "I don't need to be like you and try all thirty-one flavors to know what I like."

The irony of this is that, unbeknownst to most people, I had not tried all thirty-one flavors when it came to men.

For some reason I have never fully grasped, people have always assumed me to be more experienced in the ways of sex and dating than might be accurate. Nevertheless, she had made her point. The conversation ended. And seven years after they met, Keith proposed—at camp, where they had met those many summers prior. My mother made my sister promise she would finish her master's program before getting married, and Alisa kept her promise, scheduling the wedding for one week after graduation.

And now the big day had arrived. I took a look around the room, hoping Nette would take my cue and go torture someone else. We were all—from the bridesmaids to the mothers of the bride and groom—dressed in shades of cream. Nette and her husband, Zeit, looked like a couple out of a Fred Astaire and Ginger Rogers movie—she in a bright-white, floor-length sequined gown and he in a white dinner jacket. Truthfully, she looked like a bride in her own right. I wasn't quite sure if she had done that on purpose. It takes a special kind of chutzpah to dress like a bride at someone else's wedding, even one with a cream color scheme.

She would have stood out even without the dress. She always did. Her lavender-white hair, perfectly teased and sprayed. Her nails painted a pale shade of purplish pink that seemed to be a reflection of her hair. Her dress a gleaming white mass of sequins that floated when she moved, even if the dress might have weighed more than she did. Even at age

7

seventy-seven, her face was flawless, surgically smoothed and made-up to perfection.

"You know, we were a very liberal family to let you in, in the first place," Nette continued, taking a long pull from her martini. "I mean, me having a Chinese husband is one thing, but nothing is worse than black."

And then she took another sip out of her martini glass.

Though the bride and groom had been whisked away to take their preceremony moments alone, the room was far from empty. Among those present was my mother, who was standing within earshot. Bridesmaids and groomsmen and extended family were milling around, excited for what was about to happen. Champagne was being consumed. At Nette's comment, everyone froze and turned sharply in our direction, and every single whisper immediately stopped. It was almost as if everyone ceased breathing at the same time, awestruck that those words had come out of Nette's mouth. That any hush fell over a room filled with Jews was really something, much less at a wedding.

I hadn't been a stranger to the wrath of family members. However, when they lashed out at me, it usually happened in private—when no one was looking. Clever racists, like other abusers, like to do their work in secret, leaving bruises that only appear on the inside. Nette was the queen of the private hit. But not this time.

While it wasn't the time to make a scene, I desperately

wanted to. I wanted to scream at her. I wanted to slap her smug, painted face. I wanted to call her a bitch and a bigot. But my sister was about to walk down the aisle, and I wasn't going to let anything ruin her moment.

The weeks leading up to the wedding were not without their stresses, but they were what one would consider to be normal wedding planning stresses. My sister did not want to formally seat the guests (at her rather formal wedding), and my mother had to have a rather serious talk with her about how such things are handled. The dressmaker in charge of the bridesmaids' dresses had fallen far behind on her work, and with twenty-four hours to go, I had to give her a Don Corleone–esque talking-to about getting the dresses finished.

"My sister is getting married in one week. And I am not going to let anything ruin that for her," I told her. "We need those dresses. Tomorrow. And we need them to fit perfectly. If you need to bring your sewing machine to my mother's house, you're welcome to do that, but we will have those dresses."

Then, at the last minute, there was a change in venue for the rehearsal dinner. These normal stresses were quite welcome, given everything our family had endured the past few years.

The night before the wedding, my sister and I checked in to the hotel for a sleepover. We talked and laughed and listened to music. The next morning, my mother and the other bridesmaid joined us, and we had our hair and makeup done. In a MacGyver moment that we laugh about to this day, I even turned a hotel bedsheet into a rather fashionable wrap for my hair. It was the sweetest time, and I believed it was the perfect precursor to what was going to be an idyllic wedding.

But Nette's cruel words had just shattered my hopes of a perfect day. My mother rushed over to make sure I was still standing. I could not imagine the pain she must have been feeling. Our family was once again under attack, but this time the attacker was someone on the inside, someone who my mother loved. I excused myself. "I'll be right back," I said, trying to reassure her. My poor mother was always in a state of heightened anxiety during large family events.

"Promise me you are coming back," she implored. She knew instinctively that, wedding or no wedding, I no longer wanted to be there. My *bubbie*, the Yiddish word for grandmother, always said that weddings and funerals brought out both the best and the worst in people. I didn't want to believe that a wedding could bring out anything but the best.

"I promise. I just need a minute."

And then I went to the bar and asked for a shot of tequila. "Usually it's the groomsmen who are pounding shots before the walk down the aisle begins," said the bartender, amused. Normally, I would have smiled and flirted a bit. He was handsome, and something—someone—beautiful was exactly what I wanted in that moment. Instead, I downed the tequila in a swift gulp and let the burn of it melt away my rage.

"I'm back, Mama." I kissed her cheek, and we each took a deep breath. Still able to taste a bit of the tequila on my tongue, I put on a smile, the one I had learned to carefully place on my face as a child. I took my place. I sang. My sister got married. And my voice didn't catch on the high notes.

I was grateful that the madness had not derailed the day. Although my mother and I speak often and openly about the realities of what it has been like for our family, my sister does not. And she was, thankfully, not in the room when Nette dropped her truth on me.

"Are you happy?" I whispered in Alisa's ear when I had a moment to hug my newly married sister.

"This is the best day of my life," she gushed.

"It is the best," I said, almost choking on the words. For her, it absolutely was. And I wanted her to have that without any darkness.

At only twenty-five years old, I had already known more than my fair share of dark days. On some level, I actually respected Nette for not sugarcoating what she believed to be true. After years of being stared at and whispered about, I found it bizarrely refreshing that she was so matter-of-fact about it. And I was relieved she had finally shown her truest colors in public. But that day shattered any illusion I had left about my relationship with Nette and how she truly felt about me. And I had had many, many dreams about what a relationship with my glamorous, well-travelled great-aunt might be.

But to her, nothing was worse than black. There was no coming back from that.

The wedding reception was a blur for me. And I am a girl who really does love a good party. As I had been a part of every moment of planning the wedding, I had been looking forward to the reception. The food. The music. The speeches. The dancing. Oh, the dancing. That moment when my sister and her brand-new husband would be lifted high in the air on chairs during the hora was something I had been living for during the months of planning. And all of that was gone.

I had not a drop to drink after my preceremony tequila shot. I did my best to be present, for what could be better than seeing your sister, whom you love, marry and be so happy. It was hard for me to come back from my own brokenhearted place. I smiled and danced and helped my mother with her hostess duties, but I wasn't all there. It was supposed to be a day without this sort of ugliness—a day meant to celebrate love. The only sadness should have been when my late father's and Bubbie's absences were mentioned during the ceremony.

After the wedding, Nette went back to California and disappeared from our lives. I don't know what my mother may have said to her, and I really don't care. She was gone, and I was grateful. Life went on.

Chapter Two

OUR APARTMENT BUILDING WAS ON THE NORTH-west side of Chicago, tucked away just down the block from North Park College on a pretty, quiet residential street. The building had been in my family since Bubbie and her husband, my zayde, bought it in 1946. Like many other buildings in our neighborhood, it was a four flat, meaning it had four main apartments, with two basement units. Bubbie lived in one of the basement apartments, and we lived on one side of the first floor. Eventually, when my brother was born, we took over the other first-floor apartment, creating an enormous, light-filled fifteen-room space.

It gave us all enough room to breathe, which is important in a family with an open-door policy, like ours. Everyone was welcome—and that went for friends, family, and, at times, even strangers. As long as someone was lovely and kind they had a place at our table, and visitors were hardly unusual.

While our neighborhood wasn't particularly diverse, the makeup of our building always was. Mrs. Berg was an elderly Chinese woman who made the most delicious poppy seed cake I'd ever had. She and her adult son, Phil, lived across the hall from us. Above us, a black woman, who was a single mother, lived with her daughter. And across the hall was another single "career girl," who may or may not have been a lesbian. As long as people were polite, kind to one another, and paid their rent on time, they were welcome to live in our building.

The same was true for family. Family visits weren't just a regular occurrence at our home. They were lengthy—people didn't just come for dinner. As if our home were made out of elastic, designed to stretch to fit, we accommodated them. They came for a month. They came for a season.

Sometimes it was tremendous fun, like when Uncle Harold, Bubbie's brother, would live with us. He lived with a traumatic brain injury, which left him almost childlike. He loved me dearly and deeply. He never saw my skin color or had any concerns about my being adopted. His only concern was managing to take me down to the forbidden soda fountain at the end of our street for an ice cream sundae with rainbow whipped cream, which always managed to make me sick.

So, when I was ten and found out that Aunt Nette and

Uncle Zeit, family members I had never heard of, were coming, I had questions. Lots of questions. And, as I did nearly every day, I sat myself down on Bubbie's bed in her cool basement bedroom and asked them. Sometimes Bubbie would answer my questions, and sometimes she would not.

Bubbie was a formidable woman, both in looks and in energy. At nearly five-eight, to me she was tall, and never did I see her shrink or slouch. She stood tall at all times, even when she might have felt defeated. At a young age, I learned from her how to do the same. She had very long hair, which was pulled back into a perfect bun each day. I loved this because it allowed me to always focus on her beautiful blue eyes. Bubbie was stylish, too, mixing high and low fashion with a deftness that only truly chic women possess. And I loved her deeply.

"But who *is* she, Bubbie," I asked, "and why do we have an aunt and uncle we have never heard about or met before?"

Bubbie's eyes looked very sad. Her eyes were clear blue, like my brother's would be, and usually they were bright and warm. "Nette was my best girlfriend at school," she said. Bubbie grew up in Milwaukee with her mother, Anna, and father, Aaron Schumacher. "Nette is the person who introduced me to Alex, your zayde. Your zayde was her brother."

Bubbie was the oldest girl in her family, the third born out of five. And as seems to be the case with older siblings, Bubbie was a born caregiver. Her parents owned a grocery store in town, which kept them busy, and so my bubbie often found herself playing surrogate mother to her three brothers and younger sister—a job she did with her whole heart but one she professed she wanted to escape in favor of building a family of her own. When Nette introduced Bubbie to Alex and their romance began, she saw her opportunity to do just that. And she took it, marrying him and moving with him to Chicago, where he built his podiatry practice.

By all accounts, Bubbie told me, Alex was an excellent doctor. He was not, however, an excellent husband. He carried on a long-term affair with his secretary and was emotionally abusive toward Bubbie—and emotionally and physically abusive toward my mother. Even before she and Alex married, Bubbie's parents begged her not to go through with the wedding. They went so far as to offer to cancel it and just have a party instead. But my bubbie, stubborn and convinced that everything would sort out in her favor and, presumably, in love, moved ahead with the marriage.

Zayde died well before I was born, and unlike other family members who had passed away, he was rarely spoken of. When he was, it was never with joy or the bittersweet laughter that accompanies the loving memories of family who have passed on. For my mother and my bubbie, it was always with a tightness and a fear that outlived him. That's the thing about abuse. Its ghost lives on long after the abuser has died.

Of course, learning my late zayde had a sister I had never

known only raised more questions. "But *why* hasn't she ever come to visit?"

Bubbie told me that just as Zayde had been abusive to her and my mother, he had also been abusive to my great-aunt. He had a "race issue," and because Nette feared his reaction to her marriage to Zeit, a Chinese man, Nette kept her marriage hidden and herself safe. And part of that included not coming to Chicago.

"But we would not have cared that Zeit is Chinese, Bubbie!" I said. "Why did she wait so long? Zayde has been dead forever!" Even at ten years old, I clearly had a way with words, especially when things did not make sense to me.

"She's coming now," she said, "and that's all that matters." And that was Bubbie's way of saying she was done answering my questions for the day.

I met Nette and Zeit's luggage before I ever met them. And their luggage was gorgeous. There were seven bags, and that was definitely more bags than I had ever seen for two people. They were all different sizes and perfectly matched. Each bag had a small, rectangular tag on it with their names and address, written in what I would come to learn was Nette's graceful hand.

Then I saw them. I had never seen such an elegant couple in my life.

Nette sparkled. She sparkled like the diamonds that adorned almost all of her fingers. The only person I had ever seen sparkle like this was Dolly Parton, who had come to my grammar school in the city for a special concert. That day, I was seated on the floor at Miss Dolly's feet, as I was one of the younger students in the room. She walked out, wearing a pale-blue ruffled dress, her hair teased into an enormous blonde confection—and she sparkled. Real sparkles. Like she was covered in pixie dust. As she began to sing "Coat of Many Colors" for us, I thought she surely had to be magic and that no one sparkled in real life the way she did.

Until I met Nette.

The next thing I noticed was her hair, for it was tinted lavender. Premature grayness runs in the family, and like my mother, whose hair was fully gray by the time she was thirty, Nette's was the same. But she used a lavender rinse to make sure it never looked yellow. I don't think the lavender was meant to actually show, because when she encouraged my mother to use the rinse, my mother's hair never looked that color. I think Nette used a bit extra for dramatic effect. And it worked.

It wasn't just their travelling attire—Nette and Zeit were always impeccably dressed. He wore a suit every day, with or without a tie depending on where we were going. Nette was dressed in the highest fashion of the day, not shying away from anything. She bared her cleavage, even though she was a woman of a certain age. She wore high heels with grace. Dresses, skirts, pantsuits, even denim—Nette wore it all, and everything was perfectly tailored to fit her tiny frame, which never strayed above eighty-nine pounds.

Then there was the jewelry. So much jewelry.

We learned quickly that Nette and Zeit were travellers. World travellers. Even as a young girl, I had a sense of the gorgeous enormity of the world, and I wanted to see it all. To know that Nette and Zeit had been to places that, truly, most people only read about in books only fascinated me more. And they were doing it as senior citizens. They had been to the whole of Asia several times, including to India and Russia. And in every country they visited, Zeit bought Nette jewelry.

Her jewelry collection was like a scrapbook from each of their trips, and she did not hesitate to bring as much of it as she pleased with her. One of the smaller bags in their pile of luggage held jewelry. Only jewelry. There was costume jewelry made in the style of the host country. The pieces were made of wood, silver, beads, or adorned with filigree—and almost every piece was enormous. It was incredible. I've always found it fascinating that Nette wore the largest pieces, given how very petite she was.

The collection also contained, of course, fine jewelry, with every possible kind of gemstone represented. When they were in Thailand, Zeit bought her sapphires. She also had rubies, emeralds, and opals of differing sizes. Zeit bought her, when it was still legal, ivory and jade. And there were diamonds. Lots of diamonds. To this day, I have never seen a personal jewelry collection quite like it—and from the moment she started to pull it out of her designated jewelry suitcase, I wanted to try everything on.

That first visit, my mother, my sister, and I sat on Nette's bed, watching her carefully unpack her bags. Slowly and meticulously, as if each item were more precious than the last, she hung up her clothing, put her toiletries in the bathroom, and took out all of the jewelry to show us what she had brought.

"Alisa," Nette said, "would you like to try something on?"

A love of jewelry runs in our family, and so my sister was thrilled. "Yes!" she shouted. "Please!"

My sister had fixated on an ivory-and-black piece that must have come from China. It was a large rectangular pendant with Chinese characters on it, suspended from a thick gold chain. Nette gently put the piece over my sister's small head and turned Alisa around so that we might all admire her.

"Aunt Nette, may I try this?" I reached toward a brooch that I thought must have been made of diamonds. Her eyes were blue like Bubbie's, but sharp and cold. They narrowed.

"*No*," she snapped. "It is getting late. I am tired."

I didn't think anything of it then. My mother told Alisa to take off the necklace and suggested we leave Nette to finish unpacking in peace.

I know now that it was the very first sign I was not going to be Nette's favorite. You see, there are two things that happen when someone is trying to decide what they are going to do with you. Where they are going to put your otherness. For some, there is a blankness in the eyes that takes over, as if they are lost in thought, trying to figure out how they feel. For others, there is an immediate narrowing, a sharpness that engages. And it is because they don't need to think.

It says, before their brain can even activate, "You are not welcome here."

By contrast, Zeit took an immediate liking to me because he found me to be smart. It became apparent when I was reading by age two that I was a bright girl. But I was officially deemed a "genius" when I was IQ tested at age four to attend a special, new, experimental magnet school in Chicago. And I landed at a score of 178. By the time I met Nette and Zeit, I had already skipped three grades and was on my way to a private high school the next year. Education and intelligence were of tremendous importance to Zeit, and he was so impressed with my academic prowess that, at one point during their visit, he offered to pay for my schooling. Nette immediately ended that conversation.

"Zeit," she shouted, "you are not doing that! That is our money, and you cannot just offer it without talking with me about it." She would say this again a few years later when Zeit offered to pay for my college and graduate school. As their wealth was clear, I wondered why Nette was so un-apologetic about not wanting Zeit to be generous in any way. Bubbie said it was because Nette had grown up quite poor—at times without enough food or proper clothing—and that she always worried she wouldn't have enough.

It's a strange thing to want so badly to be close to someone who does not want to be close to you but who is working very hard to keep that hidden. But that was the dynamic set between Nette and me from the moment we met.

My mother was beside herself with excitement whenever Nette visited, because she was my mother's favorite aunt. For her, Nette had been an escape from my zayde, a man both she and Nette feared. Nette, with her unconventional lifestyle and unapologetic series of marriages, encouraged my mother to do as she had done—to forge her own path in the world. If my mother did not want to be a doctor, as her father wanted her to be, she should not have to be one. Nette encouraged my mother to be whoever she wanted to be, which was not an easy task when trapped with a man like my zayde.

My mother was three years old when she was a flower girl for Bubbie's sister, Aunt Muriel. For my mother, the best part about being a flower girl was absolutely the outfit. Isn't that always the case? Aunt Muriel had a rainbow motif for her bridesmaids, and my mother had a gorgeous frilly dress to wear, made with all the colors the older girls were wearing. And she had shoes. Very special patent leather party shoes, which were the biggest thrill of her young life. Shortly before the wedding began, Alex took my mother's beloved shoes and threw them into a furnace, right in front of her.

"Stop that crying," her father screamed, "or I will give you something to cry about."

She stopped, of course, but the damage had been done. Her beautiful party shoes were replaced with hard, black orthopedic shoes, and for her, the day was ruined. As a podiatrist, he believed that children should only wear orthopedic shoes, even if there was absolutely nothing corrective needed, and his daughter was certainly not going to be the exception to that rule, even for a couple of hours. When the story began there, the only place to go for my mother was down. As a teenager, her father conducted weekly weigh-ins and beat her if she gained a pound. And these were only the stories I knew.

We were, all of us, survivors, an unfortunate thing to have in common.

Chapter Three

THEY SAY YOU NEVER FORGET YOUR FIRST TIME; normally, that applies to when a girl makes her first purchase at Chanel or loses her virginity. On some level, that is exactly what I'm referring to. The virginity part. Not Chanel.

From the moment I was in their arms, my parents went about the business of making sure I knew I had been adopted, so it was a piece of myself that I grew up understanding. Our living room doubled as a magnificent library, filled from floor to ceiling with shelves that were, in turn, filled with gorgeous hardcover books, the kind that aren't really made anymore. Tucked away in the library was a book about adoption told using a peacock. The story spoke about a beautiful peacock that had been taken in by a group of other birds. The peacock stood out, because she did not look like the family of birds that had adopted her, but they were a family created out of love. Just like ours.

The pages were edged with gold, and they made a glorious sound when we turned them. My parents read me that book over and over again, teaching me through the pictures and prose about the poetic act of adoption. The whole of that book collection is now mine, and when I have a library big enough to unpack those precious boxes, the peacock book will be the first one I sit down to read.

Though I grew up knowing I was adopted, understanding that I was mixed race was a different story. My parents were not concerned about my skin color, and so I wasn't concerned about it. It just wasn't something we talked about. Being mixed race wasn't something *anyone* talked about in the 1970s, and as we didn't talk about it, I didn't realize I looked different from my family. That people whispered and stared was something I had grown accustomed to, but I didn't know it was my skin color that caused the commotion. I just knew that people tended to point and whisper at me. I didn't focus on the why until I was about six years old.

We knew my friend Louise and her family from the large Reform synagogue to which we belonged in Chicago. Although we did not attend the same secular school, we carpooled to religious school and often played together.

One afternoon, while playing at her house, Louise looked at me and said, "My parents say your real mother didn't want you, which is why you live with this family and you don't look like your parents."

I stopped—dead in my tracks—devastated. I had never been told my origin story in such a horrible way. And none of it made any sense to me. I had always been told that it was because I was so loved, by both my birth mother and my parents, that I had been adopted. That my birth mother knew she could not take care of me but loved me so much that she gave me to a family who could. And that my parents loved me so much the minute they saw me that they could not imagine having any daughter other than me. At no point did the story include the detail that my biological mother didn't want me. My story was that I was deeply loved.

But much like when Adam and Eve took that first bite of the forbidden fruit and learned they had been naked the whole time, so too did I learn that not everyone believed adoption to be the grand act of love I had been taught it was. To make matters worse, this was the first time anyone had ever directly pointed out to me that I looked demonstrably different from my parents. Prior to this, everything was passive-aggressive and, at least to my very young mind, a bit hazy.

Take Aunt Goldie, for example.

Goldie lived in Las Vegas, and her sense of style reflected her home city. She was loud and tacky in her brightness—sequins during the daytime, mismatched colors that screamed at you when you glanced her way. She chain-smoked, and her gruff voice sounded like the two packs she smoked per day were more like twelve. She came for a visit each year, staying for a few weeks so that she might catch up with her family.

My parents loved Las Vegas. And their yearly trip there was the only time they went on vacation without us kids. Goldie's son, Phil, was a host at the historic (and now gone) Sands Hotel and Casino at the height of its popularity, and so my parents were given the royal treatment from the moment they landed. The Sands was *the* coolest spot on the strip—or so said the Rat Pack and every other entertainer of the day. Far from high rollers, my parents were nonetheless treated to limousines, center tables, and tickets to the best shows in town. Whether it was seeing Sinatra, Steve Lawrence and Eydie Gormé, or Jubilee, my parents painted the town red as guests of Aunt Goldie and Cousin Phil, and so Goldie's visits had always been most welcome.

When my sister and I were around three and five years old, Goldie was in town visiting. We were in the backyard playing, and Goldie took my sister onto her lap to read her a book, so I came close and asked if I could sit on her other knee. "No," Goldie rasped, "but you can be a good girl and clean up my ciggie butts. Your mother and Bubbie will like that."

I did as I was told—until my mother came outside and saw what was going on. "*Marra Beth-Ann*," she screamed. I had never seen my mother's face get so red. Her nostrils flared as she continued. "What are you doing!?" It was the first time I had ever seen my mother lose it. And I wasn't quite sure why she was losing it. I had been told to do something by one of my elders, and so I was doing it.

"Aunt Goldie told me to clean it all up," I stammered, starting to cry.

"Stop that immediately—and Alisa, go into the house!"

And so she did. My mother drew me close to her, hugging my tear-stained face into her belly while she laid into Goldie with a tone of voice I had never heard before. "What is *wrong* with you?" My mother rarely speaks loudly, but she was screaming. "How could you stoop so low as to treat one of my daughters like a slave while you read a book to the other?"

My mother stopped her rant to take a deep breath. She saw how clearly upset and confused I was, and the volume of the discussion wasn't helping things. She held me tighter, and her voice dropped to almost a whisper.

"What is wrong with you, Goldie?"

At a certain point, I was also sent into the house, and my bubbie joined the argument. I couldn't really hear the words being hurled in the backyard, but afterward, Goldie packed her bags immediately, and we never saw her again. She had been told to leave, and she was not welcome back under any circumstances.

Goldie wasn't the first relative to be cast out of our family when bias had been made known, but it was the first time

I witnessed it. It was the first time I can remember knowing that something horrible was happening and that I was at the heart of it. I could not hear everything Goldie said, but I knew she was talking about me and was criticizing my parents for loving me. And I knew it was all rooted in the fact that Goldie treated Alisa differently than she did me.

As young as I was, I could feel Goldie's hatred. It was the opposite of the love I felt from my parents and my bubbie. It was palpable. Love and hate are. It was the first time I understood how deep hatred can run and how completely divisive it is. And although my mother had been born a warrior princess and had been my defender from the moment I became hers, it was the first time I saw the full breadth of her rage, strength, and unapologetically full heart. Until the birth of my brother, she had two children. And anyone who was unable to treat her daughters with the same love and respect simply wasn't welcome.

If Goldie's last visit was my first memorable experience being treated differently by someone who did not voice why, Louise was the first person to say it to my face. But I probably wasn't thinking of Goldie as I stared back at Louise. My tiny system was in shock. I did not look like my parents. How did I not look like my parents?

"Look at you," Louise said, like she could read my mind. "Your skin is brown, and your parents are white. You don't look anything like them at all."

My skin was brown. And my parents had white skin. My skin was brown. And Louise's skin was white. I saw the difference now, but I had yet to figure out—and I wanted to immediately understand—why this was a problem. I found myself reeling. I wanted to explain to her that adoption wasn't what she thought it was—that I had been both given up and taken in because I was absolutely loved. But the added kicker of being told my skin was another color threw me into complete silence. With tears streaming down my face, I ran home. I threw myself, weeping, into my mother's arms.

"She ... told ... me ... that ... the lady who had me didn't want me. SHE SAID THAT I DON'T LOOK LIKE YOU!" I wailed, almost hyperventilating.

My mother held me and calmed me down. Then, for the first time, she was forced to acknowledge that I was, in fact, different. I don't remember exactly what she said, but in that way mothers have, she made it all better. She told me that because I am different I am extra beautiful.

And then she called my father.

Up until that point, I had only ever seen my father as very kind and loving. At six feet two, he was ever imposing upon sight, but he was a gentle giant in every way. He loved to lie in bed with me on Sunday mornings and read the comics in the newspaper. He loved to try to brush and style my hair, even if it was never a successful experiment. The song "Celebration" by Kool & the Gang was his favorite, and he

31

would dance to it always—even when he believed he was alone. I had never seen rage in him until that day.

But enraged he was after my mother called him, and when he got home from work, he and my mother prepared to confront Louise's parents. I'd never heard the question, "What is wrong with people?" as many times as I did that day.

"How can parents teach their children these things?" my father asked my mother, barely containing his rage. Goldie may not have had the chutzpah to say it that day in the backyard, but Louise did—because her parents, in one way or another, had given her permission to.

But that is the thing with racism. It is taught. Carefully taught, just like the Rodgers and Hammerstein song says. It's passed down from generation to generation—like a precious family heirloom. And Louise inherited hers when we were young.

My mother and father left me at home with Bubbie when they went to speak with Louise's parents. After their conversation, the distance between our families became as big as an ocean. We stopped carpooling to synagogue. We did not acknowledge them when we saw them in the building. And Louise and I never played together again.

Goldie stopped her visits. Louise's family disappeared from our world. Racism was not welcome. From friends or family.

Chapter Four

IN THE GLORIOUS 1970S, IT WAS QUITE COMMON for sisters to be dressed alike, even if they were not twins. My mother and Bubbie fully embraced that trend, dressing Alisa and me in matching outfits. Almost all of the time. My favorite of the twinning ensembles were the Raggedy Ann dresses, complete with a tiny Raggedy Ann doll tucked into the pocket of each dress. I loved the bright red and the polka dots and the huge white bows that my mother would tie around my ponytails and on the ends of my sister's braids.

I was terribly jealous of my sister's braids. Her hair was long, shiny, and smooth. It never seemed to be knotted, as mine often was when we were brushing our hair in the morning. And it hung down her back in long, gorgeous braids, which my mother adorned with bows that matched the dress of the day. My hair, by sharp contrast, was thick, curly, and quite unruly. My mother skillfully managed to form it into ponytails, but it was never the look I coveted. I wanted my hair to look like Alisa's. Desperately.

My bubbie took a special pleasure in taking me shopping, in dressing me, and in playing with my hair. She had been as unprepared as anyone else for the arrival of her surprise brown granddaughter. But unlike many of her contemporaries, she didn't bat an eye. She never questioned my parents about why they took me. Instead, as if I were a baby Cleopatra, she bathed me in milk every week to keep my skin soft. She took me to Loehmann's and asked her favorite saleslady to bring a rack for us, and we didn't leave until it was filled with clothing. She taught me that a lady never has chipped nail polish, but she always has polish on her nails. She taught me how to cook. She let me stay up late when we had sleepovers, and we watched movies together while I lay in her soft Bubbie arms.

And she fiercely attacked anyone who dared to call her granddaughter a *schvartze*. *Schvartze* is the Yiddish equivalent of calling someone a nigger. People often try to say that it's simply Yiddish for black, but I would argue that is not true. In the 1970s, adoption and race may not have actively been a part of the cultural discourse, but name calling is an age-old game, and *schvartze* was the first Yiddish word I learned.

Like everyone else in my immediate family, my bubbie did not talk about my brownness. And she never told people

I was adopted. When I would ask her why, she always said, "No one really notices! So why tell people?"

We both knew that wasn't true. At all.

My bubbie loved me, deeply and fiercely. She must have loved me to have taken on the unenviable task of managing my hair drama.

Among the other things unique to my young life was the very special, experimental grade school I attended, Walt Disney Magnet School, the first magnet school in Chicago, opened in 1974. I was a member of one of the very first classes. It targeted gifted students, who were each tested for a minimum IQ level, but pulled the students—like a magnet—from every corner of Chicago. There were no traditional classrooms, grade levels, or grades given. Instead, students were allowed to "go at their own pace" and to retreat to the Communications Arts Center when the academic work had been completed to learn about music, dance, and visual arts. It was, for me, nirvana.

There was another adopted girl in my class at grade school named Lisa. She was black, and a white couple had adopted her when she was born. Lisa had the hair I dreamed of having. Just like my sister's. Straight, shiny, and in long braids.

"But, Bubbie," I would cry, "*why* can Lisa have straight, shiny hair that braids and I can't?"

Clearly, Lisa and her mother had some secret we did not. So, my mother called her mother and got the scoop on where they went to get help for Lisa's hair—and my bubbie made an appointment at a South Side beauty shop that specialized in hair straightening.

Then and now, Chicago has been something of a segregated city in that people of ethnic groups tend to live in certain areas. This area of the South Side in 1978 was primarily black, and for my bubbie, for the ladies in the beauty shop, and certainly for me, it was about to become a brave new world.

My bubbie was many things, but a shrinking violet was not one of them.

"Put on your best dress, Marra," she said. "It's always important to look your best when you're going to meet new people."

We dressed in synagogue finery for our trip to the beauty shop, and even before we walked in the front door, I could see the eyes of the ladies inside staring at us. When we entered, I could hear them whispering. They weren't really whispering at all.

"Who is that white lady?" said a woman by the sinks. "And why is she with that light-skinned child?" At first, I was confused. Until then, the only voices I'd heard talking about my brownness had been white ones.

"Look at her," someone else said, "wearing that big, gold, loud Jewish star . . ." My bubbie always wore her Star of David necklace, and I never thought anything of it.

Bubbie stood tall and took me by the hand, walking us to

the receptionist's counter. "We have an appointment to get my granddaughter's hair straightened," Bubbie told the woman.

The entire place smelled like hair relaxer, which at that point was made with lye. And it stank—like an even more twisted version of rotten eggs. I could see ladies in several chairs fanning themselves while their hairdressers applied the thick, white relaxer. I was terrified.

I was silently shown to a chair, and my bubbie stood beside me while my hairdresser took down my ponytails to survey the landscape. Discomfort was palpable on every possible front, but there we all were. And no one was leaving until I had silky braids like Lisa and my sister.

The hairdresser roughly applied the relaxer and told me to sit still and let it work. "It might burn a little," she said, "but you'll be all right."

The intense fire on my scalp started almost immediately, and I felt myself tearing up. Within a few minutes, the burning was so unbearable that I was crying. "Please!" I begged. "My scalp feels like it is on fire! *Please*. Take it off." Years later, when I saw Spike Lee's brilliant biopic *Malcolm X*, the scene where Denzel Washington sticks his head in a toilet to stop the hideous burn of the relaxer resonated with me. Deeply.

"Your granddaughter is tender headed," the hairdresser laughed. In truth, I was eight years old, and my mixed-race hair and young scalp should never have had the lye-based relaxer on in the first place. But there we were.

"For God's sake," Bubbie said. "She is in pain. Wash it off. Whatever it will be from here, it will be."

The cool water reduced the burning the moment it hit my head, and when all was said and done, I left the salon with silky, straight hair that would absolutely be put into long, beautiful braids. I also had burns all over my head that eventually became bleeding scabs. I'm sure there are scars. There are certainly emotional ones.

That was the day I learned that, as a mixed-race girl, there were places where my existence was not acceptable to anyone on either side of the color spectrum. At the beauty shop, I wasn't "really black" or "black enough." I was not acceptable.

My bubbie would have endured trip after trip back to that horrible shop if it would have made me happy. That's how she was. She wanted my world to be as beautiful and as normal as possible. She wanted me to be as beautiful as possible, and for the world to see me that way. When I refused to return to the site of my hair trauma, we struggled to find a way to work with my hair. In the end, my bubbie suggested we cut my very dark, tightly curled hair very short.

"Harry Belafonte's daughter wears her hair this way," Bubbie said. "She is a model. It will be gorgeous on you, mamaleh."

And so I agreed, hoping against hope that I would look like the stunning Shari Belafonte. But when I looked in the mirror, all I saw was a girl with a short Afro. And my classmates at both regular and Hebrew school wasted no time in pouncing on me, labeling me "pube head," a name that would stick well into my college years until I dared to try relaxing my hair again.

By the time I was twelve, I was already sneak-eating chocolate in an effort to soothe my young soul. Chocolate cake was my most beloved comfort, and it was most often found in my bubbie's kitchen. I would creep down into her kitchen late at night to steal a piece, hopeful that I would escape the scrutiny of familial eyes; even though they never attacked me for it, my relatives had already noted that I was starting to gain weight. My stomach became soft and full, my hips started to expand, and my breasts were already far larger than those of other girls my age. My young eyes saw only fat. I did not understand that this was simply how my body was having a bat mitzvah—transitioning from girl-hood to womanhood—just like the one I was planning with my family.

My date was August 21, 1982, and along with the anxi-ety of the event itself, and my desire to read my Torah por-tion flawlessly, came the pressure of finding just the right dresses for the occasion. Even with my self-esteem on shaky ground, shopping for my bat mitzvah outfits was the great-est joy of my young life. And Bubbie pulled out all the stops. For Friday night, there was a prairie skirt and white ruffled shirt, which was the absolute height of fashion in 1982. At least ten girls wore the same on my big day. And for the day of, we settled on a pale lavender suit and frilled, dark-purple blouse—and a pair of black Pappagallo pumps with gold trim that I wanted so badly I lied to get them.

A bat mitzvah is typically when a Jewish girl gets her first pair of high heels, and I wanted mine to be spectacular. They were at least a full size too small, and the store didn't have any in my size. "See, Bubbie," I said, cramming my feet into them, "they fit perfectly!" Eventually, I convinced her to buy them.

When we got home, I modeled each of my outfits for my family, and my parents and Bubbie told me I was perfect. I was in fashion heaven. I felt beautiful.

A couple of weeks prior to my big day, Nette arrived, and as always, she stayed in Bubbie's apartment. As Nette had always been something of a fashion goddess to me, I decided to model my outfits for her, hoping I might get her approval. I proudly put on my lavender suit, blouse, and Pappagallo pumps, and I trotted down and knocked on her bedroom door.

Nette opened the door, and without me saying a word, she surveyed me as she did every person she encountered, looking me up and down with her narrow eyes.

I quietly asked, "Do you like my outfit, Aunt Nette?"

She took a breath. "Well, you are far too young to be fat," she said. "And sloppy. A girl like you should know enough to get herself in hand, because being fat and sloppy is not going to help you in the world. And that hair certainly doesn't help matters much."

I was, it should be said, a size twelve junior at the time, and tall, strong, and curvy. (What I wouldn't give to be that size now!) I did not understand what she meant by a "girl like me." What I did understand was that, once again, I was being told I was unacceptable. My delicate twelve-year-old self—who was far more beautiful and healthier than I could have ever fathomed at the time—was ugly. And fat. And sloppy. With bad hair. She found every sensitive spot my preteen self had, and she dug in.

My mother and Bubbie, of course, were not around. And so, as had become my way, I shrank into myself. Into the space where I wanted to be invisible. I said nothing. What could I say? I left Nette's room and went up to my own, took off my beautiful suit, and had a good cry, quietly biding my time until I could find solace in my favorite chocolate-frosted friend.

Later that night, I snuck down to Bubbie's apartment to rummage for cake and saw that the light was already on. I quietly approached the kitchen, and instead of my bubbie sitting there, I found Nette. In front of her was an enormous piece of chocolate cake. She was eating it with the same sad relish I knew so well. There was no pleasure involved. There was only pain and the hope that the sweetness of each bite would make that pain go away.

We see this moment played out in films and on television over and over again—an emotional woman eating her feelings. There was an entire arc for Miranda on a *Sex and the City* episode that involved her baking a chocolate cake and proceeding to eat so much of it that she threw the rest away, only to fish it out of the trash and continue eating it.

But that is real for many people. It was certainly real for me. It was also real for Nette.

The next day, I told my mother I'd found Nette seemingly sneak-eating cake the night before. She told me Nette hid chocolate everywhere. She had it in her handbag. In her car. And in various places in her luggage. She would never eat it in front of other people, my mother said, lest there ever be a concern that she would waver from her perfect weight. She, like me, ate it in secret.

I never told my mother what Nette said to me—or that I had been on my way to eat chocolate cake myself when I spotted her. And it wasn't because I felt that I couldn't. I wanted to protect my mother from the ugliness I had experienced with Nette, just as she has always tried to do for me with other people. I did not want to be, yet again, the reason why our already small family was made smaller. In the end, of course, we cannot protect ourselves or the ones we love from the unpleasantness that others hold. But we try.

Later that day, I found myself thinking that perhaps Nette and I had more in common than either one of us might have wanted to believe. I know what caused me to eat in secret. I wondered what caused Nette to do the same. I wondered if, perhaps, she wanted to be invisible too.

Chapter Five

I REALLY DO BELIEVE WE ARE ALL MORE ALIKE THAN we are different. But I have always felt different. Been seen as different. Been called out, for better and certainly for worse, as different.

Being othered makes you extremely aware of the culture of sameness that, to me, is all around. It is the voice that dictates who is beautiful. What is fashionable. Who is important. Who can be successful.

From the time I was a young girl through my forties, I used to pray I would wake up the next morning somehow less different—a little more the same, a little less conspicuous. And yes, oftentimes that prayer included praying that I would wake up and be white, that I would look just like the other Ashkenazi Jewish girls who populated the world around me. These were the girls whom the culture of sameness deemed beautiful. Acceptable. Desirable.

I knew their families did not live with the high-powered microscope constantly pointed at them that did mine. I knew that, while they certainly had problems of their own, their problems were not like mine or my family's. We were different in every way. It was as if we lived in a fishbowl.

Our society has been damaged by the poison of racism and hate, and eventually, living under endless scrutiny warped the lens with which I viewed myself. My sense of self and beauty became tainted by these perceived differences. It has taken the whole of my lifetime to undo the damage. For me, the microscope under which I was constantly viewed wasn't limited to examining my skin color or my being adopted—or even to my being mixed race, adopted, and Jewish. It examined my whole being, and certainly my body.

I am quite the opposite of Nette, with her eighty-nine-pound, sub-five-foot frame and delicate features. While her lips were so tiny that she overlined them with lip liner, my lips are full. Her eyes were small and sharp, and my eyes are large and round. Nette's nose was also tiny, perhaps from surgery, while my nose is strongly shaped. I have ample breasts. Thick thighs. And, thankfully, even at forty-eight, I have a firm, round backside.

We were opposite expressions of the same human coin.

From the moment I started to develop at around age ten, I

have always been built this way. And, much like the unwanted attention the color of my skin brought, my shape brought with it another kind of unwanted attention, mostly from men.

I wanted to be seen the way I saw Nette being seen. People stopped her to tell her how chic and stylish she was. They called her graceful. Elegant. She walked into a room and seemed to command it—at least to my young eyes.

The way people reacted to me was clearly different. And the way men began to react to me, even at the tender age of ten, was also different.

"She is so exotic looking," I would hear men say. Exotic. Because of my darker skin and curvy young figure. Exotic. When I was at an age that I could not—and should not—understand what that meant to men.

Far beyond what is considered "normal" unwanted attention—catcalling, rude comments, leering—I attracted the attention of a man at our synagogue who considered himself a poet. He was a member of our community and was well known to be generous with the children in the religious school. He gave gifts to entire classes of students when they graduated from Hebrew school. Tie pins for the boys and Star of David necklaces for the girls.

This man, a single man who never seemed to attend services with anyone else, was a published poet. And, although I was not yet graduating, he began to give me gifts. He gave me copies of his books of poetry. "You are so beautiful," he would tell me, "so exotic. You are the reason why men write poetry, which is what I do. I write poetry for a living."

Did I mention that I was ten years old?

His poems were all about women. I knew they were romantic. But even my limited child's mind knew there was an element of sexuality in them. I thought it was odd, and so I always told my parents when this man would approach me.

"Daddy, that man at Temple gave me this book." I always gave those books to my parents.

"Thank you for telling us, sweetie. Try to stay away from him. And always tell us if he tries to be alone with you. Always tell us," my father would say.

"I will, Daddy. I promise." And I took that promise wholly to heart. I never questioned why my father wanted to keep tabs on this man. I simply knew from my father's face that this was not something to be questioned. Fortunately, I was never alone when attending services, so it was not difficult to keep my promise.

One day, this man hand-delivered to our home his newest manuscript of poems. And every single poem was about me. He wrote an entire book of poetry about his dream of deflowering my young, caramel-colored, budding, virginal body. I only had to read a few pages to know this was far bigger than anything I could manage. The shame was immediate, as was the profound discomfort. I felt dirty.

"Mama . . . ," I whispered, "you should see this."

I gave the book to my mother. She in turn gave it to my father. And we went together to the rabbi that afternoon. I cannot remember much besides sitting between my parents on the couch in the rabbi's study—fully collapsed into myself physically and emotionally.

"We will take care of this," the rabbi said. "No one who would do something like this can be a part of our community. Marra will be safe. I promise."

I knew that I was safe and that the rabbi and my parents were not going to let this man touch me. I knew that this man would never be allowed to step foot in the synagogue again. But the damage had been done. A place that should have been my safest place for so many reasons was not, and now that had been taken to a whole new level.

I was angry. Exhausted. I wanted to disappear. If no one looked at me, I wouldn't have to deal with any of this. And neither would my family. I felt responsible for the level of stress that existed for my parents because I existed. And along with that sense of responsibility came guilt.

My parents would say it was never a hardship to steer our family through these sorts of waters. There are days when my mother still goes out of her way to make sure I know there has never been a moment when she wished that things were different—certainly not that I was different.

"I do wish that people were different," she has said. "But never you."

—

I wish that some people were different too. This was never truer than when I saw my young brother have to come face-to-face for the first time, at least to my knowledge, with the cruel way that some choose to view our family.

For my brother, Merrill, being the youngest and the only son came with a set of privileges I have always envied. For starters, he never had to do anything while my bubbie was alive. He didn't have to do dishes or help clear the table. He got the exclusive use of a car while he was still in high school, and he was able to come and go much more freely and at a much younger age than my sister or I was allowed to.

"I swear to you, when I die, I'm coming back as the only boy in the family. Youngest by a decade," I have often said. "It's the greatest gig in town."

Unfortunately, his position in the family also came with a set of drawbacks. Among the most awful was that he never really got to know our beloved father. My brother was a very tender eight years old when we lost our father. While Merrill embodies our father in so many ways, he did not have the benefit of years I had to really get to know him. I see that sadness in his eyes each time someone tells him how very like our father he is.

Additionally, my brother's exposure to those who were uncomfortable with our family came very early in his life. My mother was thirty-five years old when she became pregnant with my brother, and in 1980, that was considered remarkable. Her age coupled with her beautiful, prematurely white head of hair led people to talk. And often, the talk was about whether she was his mother or grandmother.

My brother was repeatedly asked this question. And when he was, I would see his clear, beautiful blue eyes turn steely and cold. "*No*," he would say emphatically. "She is my mother."

When asked where his father was, his response was similarly curt: "He died." The answer was simple, truthful, and straightforward, as children so often are.

But one day, he was asked a new question.

I had met him as the school bus dropped him off so we could walk home together.

"Is that your sister?" asked one of his classmates.

"That is my sister," my brother replied.

"Why is your sister a nigger?"

My brother did not understand the word *nigger* because he had never heard it before. He stood there, looking at the kid on his bus with a confused but slightly angry stare clouding his bright blue eyes. I returned the young boy's taunting, arrogant gaze and gathered my brother into my arms for a hug.

"What does *nigger* mean, Marra?"

It's not often that I am at a loss for words, but this was certainly one of those times. The bus stop was at the corner of our very short block, but the walk home felt endless. We stopped on our driveway and stood under the basketball hoop before going inside. I swallowed hard and took a deep breath, and I did my best to navigate the precarious conversation.

"Well, you know how Mom and Daddy always tell us to watch our language and think about how we speak?"

"Yes . . . ," he said, only semiconvincingly.

"They say that because there are things that should never be said. Names we should never call another person. And *nigger* is one of those words."

"But why did he call you . . . that name?"

And then, differently from the way Louise had told me many years prior, I held up a mirror and explained to my brother that we didn't look alike.

And there it was. My brother had his first taste of racism.

Despite the decade age gap, Merrill and I are very close. We have always shared the same appreciation for silliness, so much so that even as adults, my mother often sits between us at family functions, and certainly when we are at synagogue, so that we will be sure to behave properly.

We speak openly about the things going on in our lives. The joys and the pain. Recently, Merrill and his wife adopted a baby girl who, being half-white and half-Latinx, is also mixed race. I have never been so proud of him as I was the day I saw so clearly that openhearted color blindness was something he inherited from our parents.

But much like our sister, Merrill rarely speaks about what

people have said to him about me beyond that day when I had to teach him what a nigger was. In their silence, I think my siblings believe they are helping to take care of me. Protecting their big sister in what ways they can.

Chapter Six

I HAVE SPENT MUCH OF MY LIFE BUILDING MY FAMILY. I chose my parents. I have chosen my friends, both when to welcome them and when it is time to let them go, carefully. Business partners too. I have tried, in vain, to choose romantic partners. And as I have built my world of kindred spirits, I have always sought guidance from those around me.

Until I learned that we are neither family nor kindred spirits, I wanted desperately to learn from Nette about the ways of men and romance. Surely she must know a great deal, I thought. No one ends up having five marriages if they don't know something.

To me, Nette was meant to be my Auntie Mame—a wholly authentic guide through the world. Her sense of style, fashion, and glamour cemented that for me. That she had had multiple husbands only enhanced the fantasy!

Ah, to be young. And foolish.

Really, what I sought was connection. And I thought that this might be a place for Nette and I to connect. After all, men seemed to be all around us both. Only later in my life would I come to understand how different, and how similar, we were in ways of men.

My mother and I often talk about marriage. When I was in my twenties, she offered her thoughts on what was important when choosing a partner, telling me that it is critically important to choose a someone who I would be happy to be with—even when the passion and sexual chemistry might no longer be there.

"I just don't understand how people your age are choosing their spouses," she sometimes says. "You live together for years, know exactly how much toilet paper the other person uses, and then divorce after four months of marriage. I married your father nine months after we met. I knew he was a good man. I knew he loved me. And I knew we wanted the same things. We worked to build a good life and a good marriage. I don't know if people do that anymore..."

She has often offered her thoughts on how one best tends to the garden of one's marriage: focus on the marriage, always, because children grow up and leave their parents, and couples that don't make their marriage the top priority—and instead focus all of their energy on their children— often end up strangers. She sees this as something lost in our generation of relationships, and she hopes that, when my time comes, I will give my marriage the care and attention it needs to thrive.

But recently she shared that, once upon a time, she had been afraid to get married. The only examples she'd had of marriages were awful ones, and she had grown up believing men were either womanizers or abusers or both, as was the case with her father. Her grandfather and uncles all had girlfriends "on the side." And then there was Nette, who had arguably been her strongest female influence aside from my bubbie, and Nette had many husbands and lovers and never seemed to be happy. There were no role models or examples to inspire my mother.

By the time I was a teenager in the 1980s, Nette and Zeit were making regular visits. Often, they would arrive together, and after a few weeks, Zeit would return to San Francisco and Nette would stay for an additional month. Sometimes two. I started to become more interested in their relationship—and Nette's past love life and what I might learn from it. And, as always, I had questions. And I drove my bubbie insane with them.

"Why has Nette had so many husbands?"

"How many were there? Really?"

"And no children? How can you have that many husbands and no children?"

"Oy, mamaleh!" Bubbie cried. "*Enough* with the questions.

I will tell you everything I know, but that's it. Now sit." She patted a place on her bed, one that had long been mine.

Bubbie told me they were just girls when Nette married for the first time, at age seventeen, as did so many girls during that time. His name was Hyman, and during her short marriage to him, Nette worked taking tickets at a local movie theater. My bubbie was already a close friend of Nette and knew this man. And when Hyman raped Nette during the early part of their marriage, it was my bubbie in whom she confided. Nette's mother fiercely held on to her Old Country ways, never learning how to speak English, and the story goes that when Nette told her mother that Hyman had raped her, her mother asked her, in Yiddish, what she had done to upset him, blaming her for the entire episode.

In an act of bravery, Nette divorced him, which was not something women did during the 1930s without true fear of being ostracized. But Nette's desire to be free was stronger than her fear, and she divorced Hyman and fled her hometown of Milwaukee, where she was considered an outcast, for Los Angeles. In the past, I have often wished that my bubbie had possessed this same bravery, but then my mother would not exist. My life, as I know it, would not have been.

Bubbie told me that Nette then became a bookkeeper in L.A., and that job eventually moved her to San Francisco, where she worked for Ralston Purina, the pet food company, and lived for the rest of her life. It was there she met George. George was a chef, and by all accounts, he was a good, hard-working man. Although Nette remained close to my bubbie, she lived in fear of my zayde, and so she did not come for visits, and they did not go to visit her in California. Zayde, like his mother, blamed Nette for anything Hyman may have done to her and did not approve of her life. At all. She was smart to stay away.

For reasons unknown, Nette divorced George. And she took a Mexican lover named José. My bubbie was the only person who knew about José, and she didn't tell me much about him that day. As my mother didn't know much of this part of Nette's romantic journey, his story died with Bubbie. That Nette took a Mexican lover fascinates me, for obvious reasons. She clearly had established a ladder of racial accept-ability, and Mexican was high enough on the list to be al-lowed into her bed, if not into her heart.

Bubbie told me that Nette eventually remarried George. In my young heart I assumed that meant she was fond of him. Perhaps even that she loved him deeply. Later, when I asked my mother if she believed Nette had loved George, my mother said, "Did Nette really love any of them? I don't think she knew how to love."

Sadly, George was not enough for Nette. Ever in fear of not having enough and still working hard as a bookkeeper, Nette wanted more. Security, in whatever way Nette defined that for herself, trumped love or the pursuit of happiness. Perhaps, to her, security *was* happiness.

Enter Vince.

Vince, Bubbie said, was a wealthy entrepreneur, and Nette smelled money on him and divorced George a second time to trade up. Vince had a large ranch in Portola Valley, California. There were horses and riding clubs. Convertibles. And Vince owned a number of businesses, which translated into a very comfortable lifestyle for them. They mingled with people like Shirley Temple, who was a member of their riding club, and they were photographed regularly for the society pages in their town.

For the first time, Nette did not have to work. She chose to continue, however, managing one of Vince's stores so that the salary would, effectively, stay in the family. She did not want money being spent on strangers when it could go to her.

Also for the first time—at least for the first time we know of—Nette openly built a love triangle. While she may have divorced George for Vince and his lifestyle, she did not let George go. Vince even gave George a restaurant to manage, thereby keeping him close for Nette. A part of Nette's security also lay in being surrounded by men who worshipped her, and this would not be the last time she asked one husband to care for the one who had preceded him.

What Nette did not know when she married Vince was that his money came from the mob. And after ten years of a marriage that seemed to have been happy, Vince divorced Nette to protect her from his debtors.

My mother lived with Vince and Nette while in college, and she was able to observe them together. She believes Vince may have been the love of Nette's life. He was the only one of her husbands to divorce her, rather than the opposite—and it was done as an act of protection. Not out of unhappiness.

Nevertheless, Nette was single again, and at some point in the mid-1960s she moved into an apartment building in Redwood City owned by Zeit Wang, who was an engineer with Lockheed. He would become her final husband, but much like her previous marriage, he was never to have Nette all to himself. Vince remained a part of Nette's life until he died. When he became sick, it was Zeit who arranged and paid for his care, and he and Nette went together to visit Vince each week until his death. To say that Nette liked to have things her way was an understatement, and it clearly extended to her marriages.

More wealthy than was Vince, with millions amassed through his hard work and clever and careful investing, Zeit was the husband who truly gave Nette the financial security and lifestyle she desired. She stopped working and took up Zeit's passion of ballroom dance. Together, they travelled the world, going on tours and cruises to every corner of the earth and on almost every continent. She was safe and well cared for, and she was denied nothing. Jewels, furs, cars. The sky was the limit, and Zeit never said no.

My bubbie and I were both exhausted by the time she finished the story of Nette's marriages. It was a lot to take in all at once. But I had asked for the whole story, and Bubbie did not disappoint. It may seem strange to think that I learned about things like love triangles from my grandmother, but Bubbie was always very open with me about very adult subjects. I knew, directly from her, about the darker parts of her marriage, and she shared those details with me before I'd become a bat mitzvah. I guess Bubbie wanted me to have a real sense of the world in as many ways as possible. And for that, I will always be grateful.

But I did feel like, at least for the moment, I understood what was about to happen next. Until it actually happened.

During one of Nette's visits, she met a man named Tom at a ballroom dance event. He was also married, but was immediately struck by Nette, and they quickly began a barely concealed affair that would last for several years. Nette's lover Tom was the reason why Zeit would go back to California and Nette would stay on with us without him.

The affair was conducted primarily out of my bubbie's apartment. Tom came and went, but we usually only saw him when he was picking up Nette to go dancing. One afternoon, Nette told us she was leaving to go shopping, and my mother and I were left to entertain Zeit.

"Uncle Zeit," I said, "would you like to play cards or something?"

We began a game of gin rummy, sitting in the cool living room of my bubbie's apartment. After a while, Nette came home, with Tom in tow, and said hello to everyone.

"Zeit," she cooed, "you remember Tom, don't you? He's my dance partner here in Chicago."

"I do," Zeit said. The two men exchanged terse pleasantries.

And then Nette and Tom retired to Bubbie's bedroom, which became Nette's when she was in town. They proceeded to have an afternoon liaison, their lovemaking loud, clear, and unapologetic.

"Mama, are they . . . ?" I started to ask. "I mean . . . those noises . . ."

"Just focus on the card game, Marra," she said, looking cautiously at Zeit.

Zeit never spoke a word, nor did he leave the room to perhaps go somewhere farther away from Nette and Tom's afternoon delight. And so we sat there, playing cards, each of us praying for different reasons that they would finish soon.

Most kids have the horrible, awkward tale about having walked in on their parents having sex. I don't have that. But I do have this.

What I now understand is that Nette used different men to fill her many different needs, often at the same time. Nette and Zeit did not have much of a physical relationship. I never saw them touch each other unless they were dancing. There was never a hand held, an embrace, or a kiss, which is strange given how intimate ballroom dance can be.

But I never saw so much as a loving glance exchanged between them. And they also had separate bedrooms, both in their home and when they travelled. It was an arrangement that seemed to work for both of them, and while their relationship may have seemed romantic on the outside, it was clearly devoid of any sexual connection.

Tom satisfied Nette's need for physical and sexual intimacy. He also seemed to satisfy her need for romance—not the material-driven kind that sat at the root of her relationship with Zeit but rather a movie kind of romance. If Zeit and Nette danced to compete, Tom danced with Nette for the intimacy and sensuality of it all. Just like in the movies.

Theirs was a very French arrangement in the midst of a very American life. And it seemingly gave Nette what she needed to be as happy as she was during her restless and unconventional life.

In spite of the freedom her husbands had given her to have relationships with other men, Nette was always convinced that her husbands were cheating on her. Always. She regularly and openly accused them of it until they would offer some gesture, usually in the form of jewelry, to make her feel secure again. Her need for material comfort was never satisfied, nor were her needs to feel secure and to be entirely in control.

When I was a teenager, Nette appeared to me to be on a seemingly inexhaustible search for love—and for the experience of being loved, Nette took four husbands in all for a total of five marriages. Of course, this desire to be loved was yet another thing Nette and I had in common but never really shared. As always, we seemed to be opposite manifestations of the same desire. Nette played out her deep need to be loved through her many marriages, but I don't think she ever believed herself worthy of truly being loved. By contrast, I have learned how deeply I deserve to be loved but have never had so much as a proper boyfriend, much less a proposal.

Most people don't know that this remains true, even now, because I have not yet been with a man who has felt comfortable bringing me home to meet his family.

When you are a unicorn, there are a thousand lies you can be fed during a lifetime.

That I was put up for adoption because no one wanted or loved me ...

That, despite my high IQ, I wouldn't amount to anything. One of my grammar school teachers believed that and told me as much to my young face ...

That my pale-brown skin is something that has to be explained ...

That I don't look Jewish ...

That black people can't be Jewish ...

The list goes on and on.

One of the most poisonous lies I have ever been told was that no man would ever be comfortable enough with my otherness to take me home to meet his family. And many a man has told me that tale.

The funny thing is that I am, at heart, a romantic. I have often joked that I am the reason why the old-fashioned Broadway musicals exist. Boy meets girl. Boy gets girl. Boy loses girl. The orchestra swells—and then boy and girl kiss and ride off into the sunset. But at some point during the courtship, boy brings girl home to meet his family.

To bring someone special out to meet your friends, to meet your family, is universally known to be a sign that things are serious. Committed. Proud. And, much like other seminal moments of harsh reality, I was told first by a male friend when I was about twenty-two years old that I shouldn't expect to have this experience. At least not with a nice Jewish boy.

Joe and I had grown up together from the age of ten. We went to my beloved summer camp, then to youth group, and then to college together. He was a part of a group of boys who were among my closest friends. I had never dated or even made out with any of them. Rather, I was "one of the guys." The rare girl in whom they confided. Talked with about other girls. Asked for support and comfort. Needing the same, I turned to Joe on the heels of a devastating encounter with a boy named Ron.

Ron was someone I had known since my college days, and in our immediate postcollege life, we sat on the same Jewish charity board for young adults. Our social circle was small, and our socializing almost always amounted to making the rounds at the most popular bars or going to parties. Ron, then in medical school, started to show up at all of the places where I was partying. He would often walk me to my car. Ask me to dance. He even brought me flowers on the night of one of our board meetings.

"When are you going to finally ask me out?" I asked him one night. "You know. Take me on a date?"

Ron grew immediately uncomfortable, and the silence told me I was absolutely not going to like what he had to say.

"I think you're brilliant," he said finally. "And beautiful. And funny. And kind. And wonderful and amazing. But I can't take you on a date because I wouldn't know how to explain you to my family."

I did not understand. Perhaps I did not want to understand. So I simply said, "Why?"

And he took a deep, pained breath and said, "Look at you. How could I explain your skin color to my parents?"

I felt the rage and the hurt well up as quickly as the tears did. I launched into an immediate listing of all of the things about me that made me, I thought, the perfect nice Jewish girl.

"For goodness' sake," I cried, "I speak Hebrew. Fluently!"

And he agreed that while all of that was true, he would never be able to get his family comfortable with me.

Brokenhearted, I went to Joe for comfort. I expected him to say to me what I had always said to him when the current girl of his dreams had proved to be far from dreamy: that it was Ron's loss. That he was being racist and stupid. But instead, Joe said quite the opposite.

"In the name of our friendship," he began, "I feel it is my obligation to tell you that you shouldn't expect to find a Jewish boy to marry." I hadn't thought anyone could dumbfound me more than Ron had. But Joe continued. "We have talked about it. And you *are* smart, funny, and pretty, but Ron is right. You are too complicated to bring home. Jewish girls don't look like you, and I just don't see any guy feeling comfortable bringing you home to meet his family."

Even with the tears visibly swelling in my eyes, he pressed on and spoke the words that brought it all home.

"I mean, a lot of us would love to sleep with you. We've talked about it. But that's where it would end. And I don't want you to delude yourself into thinking there would be anything more."

Racism wrapped in the guise of friendship is perhaps one of the cruelest forms.

Oddly enough, I had been told something similar by a black man not long before that. He, like Ron, seemed to be following me around in a similar fashion. One afternoon when we were chatting, however, one invitation blew up his entire understanding of who I am.

"Would you like to join me at church this Sunday?" he asked.

"I would be happy to go to church with you," I replied, "but you should know that I am Jewish."

"I don't understand . . . ," he said. "Why would you *choose* to be Jewish? You're black! Black people are not Jewish! Maybe Muslim. Definitely Christian. But *not* Jewish."

There it was. Jewish boys didn't want to explain my brown skin. And black boys could not understand or embrace my Judaism. I was good for sex, but even that would only happen in the shadows. Wanting me in any way was, it seemed, a dirty little secret.

During much of my twenties, the men who approached me were only interested in sex. But with the advent of internet dating during my late twenties and early thirties, I thought I would surely be able to find the One. So many of my friends had been successful with it that I decided to give it a go.

I put up a profile on JDate, an online dating site aimed at the Jewish population, and settled in to see what came back. While my profile did not speak to race, my photos spoke a thousand words. The responses were overwhelming. Men from all over the country wrote to me, saying they found me to be beautiful, exotic, intelligent, and fascinating. Much like my profile, they did not speak of race either. They simply came to me. From all over the world.

While my friends were often taking first dates for coffee or for a drink, for me, it was always an invitation to dinner—and I was usually taken to one of the more expensive restaurants in town. They were doctors, attorneys, studio executives, and business owners. At times, I had so many offers for dates that I had two or three in one day.

And I ate it up.

I hoped that dating this actively would fill the many holes in my terribly wounded heart and soul. I believed one of these men might turn out to be the great love of my life. Deep down, I also hoped that if I married a nice Jewish boy like the rest of the girls I knew, it might lessen my sense of being "other" in my own community. It might make me, even in some small way, more acceptable than most people found me to be.

But rarely was there a second date. There was dinner. A grand charm offensive. And then the full-court press for a sexual sort of dessert. One night, on one such date with an attorney from San Francisco, enough wine had flowed for me to have the courage to ask him directly why on earth he elected to hop a flight to Chicago for a date.

"Surely," I said, "there are plenty of suitable options in California."

And, as the wine had loosened his tongue as well, my

suitor replied without even a hint of delicacy, "Are you *kidding*? I had to come. I've never met a Jewish girl who looks like you, and let's face it: Jewish boys have jungle fever."

Jewish boys have jungle fever.

To these men, I was like a movie character. Perhaps not real. Definitely unusual. And absolutely something to see. To see, but not to truly experience. Not to really get to know. I was . . . a conquest.

I have cried myself to sleep many nights. Wept to my mother. To close friends. Prayed from the deepest place in my heart that my openhearted, open-minded prince would come. I even considered, at one naive point in my young life, talking to Nette about it. She had taken so many husbands that perhaps she held a secret that might help.

Thank goodness I didn't. Not because she was so hateful to me, but because I now know that she was the last person to seek guidance from in the ways of men. Or love. An abuser—and racism is absolutely abuse—cannot possibly be that guide. I knew how she felt about my weight, and I certainly came to understand how she felt about my looks and the color of my skin. What more did I really need to know? Other than, of course, that I might be a lesbian because I was dateless at Alisa's wedding.

Chapter Seven

LATE 1989 BEGAN A DARK PERIOD FOR MY FAMILY. One filled with illness, pain, and death. To watch anyone die is both an honor and a horror. To watch a beloved family member do the same is a privilege. But when those who are leaving are among the few people who you know love you fully—unconditionally—and without reservation, it is terrifying.

"Something is wrong with Daddy," my mother's never-wavering voice said over the phone. They had been at the Labor Day parade. I was never one for such things, but my parents loved it, and as Labor Day falls near my mother's September 2 birthday, the parade was often how the celebrating began. That September, I was home from my final semester at the University of Illinois at Urbana-Champaign. And I had mono. I was still a bit sick and desperate to get back to school; the parade was the last place I wanted to go.

"Daddy's face is frozen, so I'm taking him to the hospital. I'm sure it's nothing," she said. "You stay at home with Bubbie and your brother. I'll call you as soon as we know something. We love you. Everything is going to be fine."

"I love you too," I said. "Give Daddy a kiss from me and please tell him to listen to whatever the doctors tell him to do."

He had undergone a complete physical just a couple of months prior, during the summer, and had been proclaimed healthy as a horse, so we were all hopeful.

"Everything will be fine."

Hours and hours later, the word came back.

"Daddy has some kind of leukemia. But everything is going to be fine. The doctors aren't concerned. He's in excellent hands."

But it wasn't a common kind of leukemia. My father had acute prolymphocytic T-cell leukemia, a very rare form that tends to afflict middle-aged Ashkenazi Jewish men. And there was no known way to cure it or put patients into remission.

My father was immediately hospitalized, and for the bulk of the next four months, he remained in the hospital. Since I was just getting over having mono and his immune system was compromised, I was not allowed to visit during the very early days. He spent his days getting prodded and tested by doctors, and I spent mine trying desperately to cope with totally foreign territory. I simply wanted to see him. To kiss his cheek. To sit in the room with him. But that was not going to happen, and neither one of us was faring well.

I was sent back to school to finish the semester, and everything was different. Education was critically important to my father, and so we all did our best, me in my senior year of college and my sister in her freshman, to carry on.

Back then, cancer didn't seem to be nearly as prevalent as it is today. I did not know anyone who had lost a parent or a sibling to any disease at that point. I only knew people who had lost grandparents to understandable old age; I had also heard stories of tragic accidents that had taken people suddenly and far too soon. I didn't know anyone who had gone through what I was going through . . . or who *was* going through what I was going through. My brother, at only eight years old, was far too young to talk to about things, and my sister was at the University of Iowa, trying to get through her first year of college with this looming over her.

I didn't know how to talk about it. But, really, I didn't know how to talk about much back then. I did not know how much I could or should share with even those who I considered to be my closest friends. We didn't talk about the fact that I was three years younger than anyone else at the university, that I was mixed race in a very white world, that I was both brown and Jewish, or that I was adopted. Why on earth would I share this? That I was terrified? Not just for my father, but for all of us?

I didn't know how to speak any of my truths back then.

Instead, I spent my time rehearsing for the fall musical and going back and forth to Chicago so that I might spend as much time as possible with my father and my family. I frantically researched leukemia and alternative methods of healing, and in my desperate naiveté, I even bought my father an aloe vera plant, which I had read had great healing properties. I would have done or tried anything to help, even if the help was through the comedy of a beautiful yet useless plant for his hospital room.

The next five months were excruciating. After a particularly scary time in January 1990, including an emergency bowel resection and an extended stay in intensive care, my father was released to rest comfortably at home. Having graduated the previous December, I had moved back into the house, and one evening my mother left me to keep an eye on my father while she went to the grocery store.

"I'll be back in just a bit," she said. "We need a few things from the store. Everything will be fine."

It was terrifying to be all of nineteen years old and to see what leukemia had done to my brave, strong father. The disease ravaged him, leaving barely one hundred pounds on his six-foot-two frame. His hair was gone, as was his once voracious appetite, but he remained very much himself. Loving, funny, sweet—and absolutely stubborn.

Despite my mother's calm, even assurances, I was

nervous. She took my brother with her, and my father and I settled in to watch television. Being around my father typically brought me nothing but joy. I could never have imagined being nervous around him until that night. And I'm quite sure my forty-seven-year-old father could not have imagined his teenage daughter having to babysit him, which made it uncomfortable for both of us.

But there we were.

Not more than fifteen minutes after my mother left, my father began to bleed. It seeped all over the recliner chair in which he sat and onto the floor, and I could see what little color he had in his face begin to fade. I had never seen that much blood, and I pray I never see it again. I reached for the phone to call 911, and my father started to scream and cry, all the while with the color and life draining from his body.

"Please do not call an ambulance, Marra! Please," he begged. "I want to die at home. Here. Please don't let them come for me."

I could not let that happen. I could not let him die in our house.

"I'm so sorry, Daddy . . ."

I put down the phone and lifted him out of the chair—amid his screaming and crying—and I put him into my car and drove him to the hospital. To this day, his screams haunt me. Of all the things I have endured, this has always been the worst night.

When we arrived at the hospital, they took him away to stop the bleeding, and I waited for my mother. "Mama . . . ," I said when she arrived, "I couldn't let him die at the house. I just couldn't. I didn't know what to do . . ."

"Shh," she whispered to me. "You did the right thing."

"Even if it wasn't what Daddy wanted?"

"Even if it wasn't what Daddy wanted," she said. "Don't worry. I'll be right back."

I was sent home to be with Bubbie and my brother. My poor little brother, who was so young and so tired. I pray he doesn't remember this night. He always tells me he doesn't remember much from that time. I wish I could forget some of it myself.

I came back the next day and found my father awake but drugged out of his mind on morphine. I wanted to apologize for defying him and for taking him to the hospital, but instead I pulled a chair next to his bed and we talked about salmon fishing.

"I want to do the helicopter kind, Marra," he said, "where they fly you out to a remote place and leave you there. To fish, and sleep outside. That's the kind I want to do. In Alaska."

My father never indulged his desire to go salmon fishing because he never felt it was more important than doing all he could to give us absolutely everything. So he put the trip on his "someday" list and instead took us to Disney World— which was something for the entire family to enjoy. He paid in full for my sister and me to go to college so that we could focus on our studies and not feel pressured to have a job while in school. An accountant by trade, he always worked hard, but when he developed a degenerative eye disease and was no longer able to continue in accounting, he took on two warehouse jobs at the same time to ensure that my mother could stay home with us. And he did it without complaint. My father was one of the most truly unselfish souls I have ever known. My mother is equally selfless.

"I'll tell you what, Daddy," I said. "When you get better, I will go salmon fishing with you. The helicopter kind. I'll sleep outside. I'll wear the horrible outfit. The rubber pants. All of it. I'll do it. As soon as you're better, we will go. I'll go to the library tonight and get some books, and we can start researching our trip."

I knew that "someday" probably would never come, but I thought it might take his mind off things to plan the trip. I'm guessing it was my willingness to wear the waders that brought a sleepy, stoned smile to his face. My father knew well how much I love a good outfit, and he knew that for me to offer to sleep outside and wear waders was a supreme act of love.

My mother, who had been sitting in the corner listening to our talk of fishing, was called out of the room to speak with his doctor, and so once again, I was left alone with my father. I wasn't nearly as afraid this time. I mean, what could possibly happen now?

"I need some water, Marra."

He was unable to lift his head, or even the glass, and since he did not want to use a straw, I was tasked with trying to pour the water into his mouth—without spilling it everywhere. And I failed. Miserably. I soaked his hospital gown and the pillow.

"Why can't you pour it into my mouth like your mother does!" my father, soaked and now cold, yelled at me.

I don't know what possessed me to do it . . . but I yelled back.

"Because I can't!" I cried. "And you now have three choices. You can wait for Mom to do it, you can use the straw, or you can do it yourself. And that clearly isn't an option!" When I realized I was yelling at my father, I became silent and sat down. Horrified.

And my father began to laugh. He laughed harder than he had in weeks. And he took my hand and said, "Oh, Marra. Only you would yell at a dying man . . . and get away with it."

This was the only time during his illness that he actually acknowledged out loud that he was dying. Only my beloved father could have found humor in such a moment.

I was sent home, with kisses from both of my parents, to again be with my bubbie and my brother. This time, it was to wait.

"I'm going to stay here with your father until it's all over, Marra," my mother told me. "I'll call you and tell you that

I'm ready to be picked up. And when I do, you'll know. So stay by the phone. And always answer the other line if you're talking to someone else."

The phone rang at least twenty-five times that night, and each time, my heart stopped. But I did as my mother asked. I was talking with my best friend, Harry, when the call came in.

"I don't want to answer it," I said.

"You have to," he said, gently. "It could be your mother."

And it was. Ready to be picked up from the hospital.

She had not left his side for those final hours, and when I arrived, she gave me time to say my goodbyes.

"Daddy, please . . . wake up," I said. "Come back to us. We need you. I need you. Wake up, please . . ."

But he was gone. My beloved, hilarious, loving, hard-working father was gone. I tried so hard to wake him up, sitting in the room with his lifeless body for nearly an hour before my mother gently peeled me away to take me to a home that would never again be the same. He was gone, and with him, one of my greatest protectors from a world that was so often unkind.

I confess I have blocked most of this from my otherwise considerable memory. I could not conceive of a world without him there to love me, to teach me, to make me laugh. To protect me, as he did in every moment, even when we were not together.

My friends, utterly ill equipped to deal with my grief,

nonetheless came from Champaign to Chicago to try to be of help. It is Jewish custom to bury the dead as quickly as possible, so there were only three days between his death and the funeral. One afternoon, after we made a strong pitcher of Long Island iced tea for my mother in an effort to force her to get some much-needed sleep, my friends managed to get me out of the house.

We went to what was then my nirvana: the mall. We had lunch and ice cream at the Claim Company, and I found myself smiling for the first time in what seemed like a year. Then we headed to the record store. FAO Schwarz, the toy store, was on the way, so I stopped in to see if there might be something to bring back for my brother. As I browsed, an older, white, and presumably Jewish saleswoman approached me.

"Why are you wearing that?" she said, gesturing toward my torn black ribbon. "That is a sign of *mourning* for *Jewish people*! You should not be wearing that!"

She was right. It is Jewish custom that we wear the ribbon over our heart for thirty days as a visible sign of mourning when an immediate family member, such as a father, has died. Orthodox Jews actually tear their clothing.

Instinctively, I looked around for my father. But he was not there to step in. There was only me. "I am Jewish, too," I stammered, "and we recently lost my father. So I *am* in mourning."

But she could not hear me. Or perhaps she would not.

My friends saw what was happening as they walked up and dragged me out of the store. Even during the worst time of my young life, I was apparently not going to get a respite from the hostile, public, and constant questioning of my very existence. And now, I had one less shield against it all.

We went to the record store, and my friends bought me my first Etta James album. "Etta James will cure what is ailing you, sweetie," cooed Harry.

We returned to the house, finished what was left of the Long Island iced tea, and lay on the living room floor to listen to Miss Etta sing: "I want a Sunday kind of love . . . a love to last past Saturday night."

She was singing bittersweet love songs on this album, but her voice went straight through to the core of my broken heart. And to this day, Etta James's music offers a unique comfort whenever I am in need. I always found it more than a bit painful that we also lost her to leukemia some years later.

My mother elected to have my father's memorial service at our house. This was a marked departure from a traditional Jewish funeral on a number of levels. First, my father had been cremated, which was something previously not done by Jews as a rule. Reform Jews, which we are, had just begun to embrace the practice. Second, a Jewish funeral would typically be held at a synagogue or in the chapel at a funeral home or cemetery.

But my father loved the house, and I think having the service at home made my mother feel closer to him at a time when he could not have been further away. And for my siblings and me, it was a comfort to be at home.

Once again, my friends came. And I, conditioned to always be graceful, did my very best to make them feel comfortable by not letting them see me cry. I knew that they were coming to support me, that they were there to stand by me on my darkest day. To love me. But, ever aware of people's discomfort, I did not want to show anyone the true depth of my pain—even my closest friends.

Armed with fashion as a litmus test, Harry arrived in a hideous sport jacket, purchased at the Salvation Army in Champaign for the occasion.

"What are you *wearing*?" I exclaimed when I answered the door.

My response elicited smiles and uncomfortable laughter from my friends. They knew that if I commented on the jacket, I was still alive inside. To this day, I remain grateful that he wore something so ugly, for the sight of it brought me back to myself. Nothing draws a girl out like an otherwise impeccably dressed gay man in an intentionally, comically bad outfit. At a funeral.

Our much-beloved rabbi was amazing—and he brought with him the tenderness, peace, and love our family so desperately needed on that day. After he finished the traditional

Jewish funeral prayers, and once the mournful sounds of *El Malei Rachamim* had ended, Rabbi added yet another unique touch to the day by sharing a personal story about my father. He spoke in his calming voice about how gentle and affectionate a man my father was. And that he'd seen my father's gentleness manifest most when he was at synagogue with his family. That he always seemed to be holding the hands of his children. He always made sure to escort my mother to every place she went.

And then the rabbi asked our friends and family to join him.

"I'd like to invite anyone who would like to, to also share a story or a memory about Jerry. In this way, we can celebrate his life together and offer comfort to his family."

The rabbi's invitation was meant to be a celebration of my father and the wonderful, loving man that he was. It was meant to fill our hearts with the joy of his memory on an impossible day. I was sitting on the floor at my mother's feet during the service, and as the stories began, I was feeling everything the rabbi wanted us to feel. Comforted. Loved. I understood that my father had been loved deeply during his life and that we were in a room surrounded by people who wanted us to celebrate the life of a loving, kind, funny, and special man.

When it was my turn, I quietly wrapped my arm around my mother's leg and breathed in.

"My father always told me that he wanted to keep me in a glass cage so that I would always be able to see the world but would never be hurt by it," I said. "In so many ways, he was my glass cage. My ever-present protector. There are no words for how much I loved him. Or how much I will miss him . . ."

I glanced around the room and noticed a few members of my father's family. We never had much of a relationship with that side of the family, but my father wanted them to be invited. "Marra," he had said, "I want you to call them and tell them I'm sick. Tell them I want to see them." I had asked if someone else could make the call, but he said no. "I want it to be you," he had said. "Please." And so I had called and introduced myself to a grandmother I barely knew. And here they were.

"Your father gave up everything for *you*," one of them raged, turning his sights squarely on me. "I just hope you were worth it."

And in that moment, my glass cage shattered.

I could not escape the brand of racist hate that had been hurled at my family and me from the moment we found one another. Even at my father's funeral, there was no escape. I would love to know what my father would have said. But he was gone, and instead, there was silence.

In a room filled with family, friends, and my father's coworkers, you could have heard a pin drop. I opened my mouth to speak—for the first time when confronted like this—but I felt my mother's hand on my shoulder, heard the gasps that had overtaken the room, and saw a college friend shake his head as if to say, "Now is not the time."

And so instead, I said nothing and let Rabbi somehow bring us back to a place of focus and peace—and recover the state of grace that had just had a bomb dropped on it.

We finished the service, and my father's family mercifully left immediately afterward. We moved on to the *shiva*, and I did my part and let people tell me how sorry they were and how much my father was loved and would be missed. But I wasn't really there after my glass cage was shattered. My sister decided to stay upstairs with our mother, and I withdrew to the basement with my little brother and my friends, where we played video games and ate the chocolate chip coffee cake I had managed to tuck away when all of the food arrived.

Chapter Eight

ALMOST IMMEDIATELY FOLLOWING MY FATHER'S death, my bubbie became quite ill. If I look back in my memory banks, I don't remember a time when she wasn't sick. Whether it was her Hashimoto's disease or her heart condition, my bubbie was a combination of spirit strong and body broken for much of my life. This time, though, it was ovarian cancer, which was odd given that she had had a full hysterectomy years before. Apparently, even the tiniest bit of tissue left in the body can become a place for cancer to grow. And it did.

When I was around thirteen years old, she started to prepare me for her inevitable death. "I'm going to die someday, mamaleh," she would say. And I would always respond, "Bubbie, I'll let you know when it's time for you to go. I promise."

A bit macabre, I know, but it was nonetheless a part of our repartee. There were many times when our interactions were both macabre and funny. That was the beauty of her. She was always able to make even the most horrible moments somehow palatable.

Much like my father, she took on the role of protector, especially on the rare occasions when we had to deal with my father's family. When his relatives arrived at the hospital during his illness, my bubbie became filled with the love and rage that only she could pull together. She took me by the hand and dragged me out of the room, as if I were a young child.

"*They* will *never* see *my* granddaughter," she proclaimed. "Come, mamaleh. Let's go get some ice cream."

Only my bubbie would have made that kind of scene and then turned on her heel to take me for ice cream. And only she could have made it work. Like something out of a movie.

As it turned out, things went so badly that the hospital asked my father's family to leave and my father had to be sedated. To this day, I don't know what was said, and no matter how I try to get it out of her, my mother will not speak of it. I only know that I wasn't there to witness it because of my bubbie and our trip for ice cream.

I spent the two years after my father's death doing my best to become a star in the world of Chicago musical theater. After losing him, I wanted nothing more than to lose myself by playing characters that were not me. It seemed the perfect escape from my profound grief. Unfortunately, the early 1990s did not provide the warmest and most open environment for mixed-race casting, and few directors knew what to do with me. For better or worse, I once saw the director's notes on a casting sheet: "Is she black or is she white? What do we do with her?" Questions that some ask to this day.

I found a space doing original works of theater and joyfully did every rock opera that welcomed people who don't fall neatly into any one category. Shows like *Hair* and *Jesus Christ Superstar* offered me a place. I was never going to be in *Oklahoma!* or *Fiddler on the Roof.* And I knew it. But that did not stop me from trying, and I certainly brought my flair for the dramatic home with me, something that my bubbie enjoyed.

Bubbie was hospitalized for the final time in late June 1992, just before the famous Taste of Chicago festival began. For more than a decade, the Taste had been *the* way to celebrate the Fourth of July in the city, and this was my year to go. I had never been and had made big plans. But Bubbie didn't want me to go.

"I don't like crowds. You don't need to go," she said.

"But, Bubbie, it looks like it's so much fun! Don't you want me to have fun?"

And then, while I was making plans to attend in spite of Bubbie's wishes, we came to understand these were going to be her final days. I saw how tired she was, and I did as I had promised I would do. "Bubbie, I promised you I would tell you when it's time for you to go. And I think it is time."

She smiled at me. "Mamaleh, you did promise me you'd tell me. You're a good girl. Thank you. But I still don't want you to go to the Taste of Chicago."

I laughed. "If I know you, you'll wait and die on the Fourth of July just to make sure I don't ever go!"

And that is exactly what she did. I believe it was on purpose so that she could leave me with a reminder of the truly comical character she was.

Unlike when my father died, I was present during her final moments. This time, I didn't leave my mother's side. I was grateful to be with them. It is a remarkable thing to be there when a life comes into the world, and it is equally remarkable to be there when a life leaves the world. I am privileged to have experienced both.

My bubbie was put on a morphine drip, which we were told would "slow her body" so that she might drift off into a permanent and peaceful sleep. Unfortunately, that is not how it worked, and she ended up holding on, with her heart unwilling to stop beating, for several days. The rest of her body was already gone, including her brain, and she had turned blue. I had never seen anything quite like it. My mother, who had been quiet and very composed during my father's illness, was beside herself. Seeing her in so much pain was almost as bad as knowing that my beloved bubbie was on the verge of death.

"I don't understand why you can't turn up the drip!" my

mother wailed to the doctor. She begged the doctor to do something—my bubbie clearly had not been given enough of the drug for a peaceful send-off. The nurse agreed that the dosage needed to be adjusted to better do its work. But the doctor did not.

I joined in. "What is wrong with you, Doctor? Can't you see that she is suffering? *Please*," I begged, "increase the dosage like the nurse said you can so that this might all be over."

"You are a horrible, selfish person to want to use a drug in this way," the doctor shouted at me. "You just don't want to have to watch it, but this is what death looks like."

With the same brand of fierceness and protection that my bubbie had long shown to me, I decided to take matters into my own hands, and once the doctor left us alone, I went to turn up the morphine myself. By then, I had spent enough time in hospital rooms to know exactly what to do. But my mother stopped me. "Please, Marra," she said. "They'll send you to jail. Don't do this. I can't lose you too."

And so we waited. Locked away in the room with my bubbie's blue body and her strong heart. It's amazing, really, that it was her heart that held on for so long. Clinically, it had always been considered weak. That could not have been further from the truth.

Finally, at some point on the Fourth of July, she left us. I did not go to the Taste of Chicago, and to this day, I have never been, and I do not celebrate on the Fourth of July. But

I do laugh knowing that my bubbie got the final word—just as she would have wanted.

When families go through losses, people come. They pay their respects. They hover. And people came, both when my father died and again when my bubbie did. However, Nette was conspicuously absent, even though she and my bubbie had been close since their grammar school days. In retrospect, I think it was because Nette liked a party. And no matter how delicious the food at a *shiva* might be, it is not a party.

What she did do was try to help soothe the pain for my mother by taking her on trips. Typically, they went on cruises. It was one of the ways Nette showed her love and affection for my mother, and no matter what else I can say about her, Nette did love my mother as if she were her own child. Or, at least, close to it.

Nette also felt that we should come to San Francisco to spend time with her. And by "we," she didn't mean me. She meant my siblings.

Chapter Nine

NETTE SENT A PLANE TICKET FIRST FOR MY SISTER. While I don't remember much about the details of her trip, I do remember that Alisa came home with a beautiful garnet birthstone ring, which Nette and Zeit had bought for her. She wears it to this day, and I know it was very special for her to shop for it with them.

Never afraid to ask for what I want, I began to do what I do best: ask questions. "Aunt Nette, when will it be my turn to come?" I said. "I've never been to California, and Alisa said I will love it."

"We need a long break between visitors, Marra."

"You're so busy doing other things, Marra."

"We will work it out later, Marra."

A later that would never come.

Next, Nette sent for my mother and my brother. As my

brother was significantly younger than my sister and me, it was more comfortable for Nette and Zeit—and, I suspect, my brother—to have my mother present, and Nette was always happy to spend time with my mother. Again, plane tickets were furnished for them, and they had a lovely time.

One of my favorite sayings is "If the door does not open for you, it's not your door." It really is like hitting your head against a wall: painful and ill-advised. And as a girl who has spent her life quite literally begging to be seen—to be given a chance, to be liked, loved, wanted—I have also spent a lifetime knocking on the wrong doors. It took a long time, but I came to understand that I must stop wanting the people who don't want me.

Never did I knock harder than on Nette's door. And perhaps the pinnacle of that was my choice to fly myself to San Francisco and force a visit with Nette and Zeit.

My mother had begun to ask Nette when I would be sent for, and the litany of vague responses continued. "Oh, Ellie, don't make such a big deal out of it," Nette would say. "Marra will come when it's the right time."

And as Nette was clever and did not behave in the overtly racist ways that Goldie had—or call me *schvartze* under her breath as other relatives had—the conversation with her became a bit more complicated than were other ones. In retrospect, I suspect we both knew what her issue was. We just did not want to talk about it.

During the summer after my bubbie's death, I was planning to be in L.A., and so I scheduled a stop in San Francisco and called Nette. "I'm spending the summer in Los Angeles, working at a summer camp there," I told her, "and thought I would fly up to San Francisco first to visit you."

"Well...," I heard hesitation in her voice. "We have a very busy schedule..."

"I won't stay long, don't worry," I said. "And I'm buying my own ticket." I completely debased myself without giving it a second thought, and I did not give her any space to say no.

"Well, I guess we can find thirty-six or so hours for a visit," she replied, "but no longer."

My hopes, as ever, were high that this would be the moment Nette would come to really embrace me. That perhaps some quiet time alone would be enough to show her that we had a lot in common. I wanted to hear absolutely everything she had to tell me about her travels. About her ballroom dancing. About her romances. About her jewelry. About her life.

But from the moment Nette and Zeit picked me up from the airport, it was clear that the visit was not going to be nearly as romantic as I had dreamed it would be—and that Nette had little interest in doing anything special with me while I was there.

I came armed with a list of things my sister had enjoyed doing and took the liberty of asking if we might stop for lunch in Sausalito, which Alisa had said was just gorgeous.

Deep inside, I'd known even before I'd booked my ticket that this trip was probably not a good idea. But, in my typical type A fashion, I wanted to get ahead of things. In my mind, having more planned time and less downtime would be a good thing—less potential time for awkwardness.

"I have things I need to do for myself, Marra," Nette said. "I don't have the time or energy to run you all over the place."

Zeit, who had always been kind to me, noted my disappointment, and so he tried to find a way to create balance. "Why don't we spend some time walking through the shops after lunch?" he said. "Nette, you love these shops . . ."

We wandered the main street of the town, going in and out of jewelry stores. Surely, I thought, Nette will offer to buy me a piece of jewelry as she did for my sister. I was not subtle in talking about how much I loved jewelry, commenting on the pieces Nette was wearing that day.

"Is this where you bought Alisa's ring?" I asked in one store. "It's so beautiful. And I really love the one you're wearing today, Aunt Nette."

Flattery was getting me absolutely nowhere. And so, I swallowed what was left of my, at that point, nearly non-existent pride and asked directly for what I wanted. "I would love to have a ring like Alisa's," I said. "It would mean so much to me coming from you and Uncle Zeit." For me to have a gift from Nette would mean that, even in some small way, she at least cared for me a bit. Or so I foolishly believed.

Nette, who was focused on the jewelry she wanted for herself, did not say anything.

Then we went into a store that sold fire opals. I was mesmerized by them. "These are the most incredible stones I have ever seen! The colors dance!" Boldly, I continued to speak. "I want a ring with one of these stones in it."

There was yet another moment of awkward silence as my words hung in the air and Nette stared at me coldly. "I suppose I could buy you a little something . . . ," Zeit began. But Nette stopped him immediately.

"If you're going to buy anyone jewelry, it's going to be *me*. Not *her*."

They had, as they often did, a bit of an argument, and I stood alone, looking down into the cases and trying not to cry. It was absolutely humiliating on every possible front to stand there, listening to them argue about why Zeit wanted to buy me something—and why Nette would not allow it. It was more humiliating to realize I had done all of this to myself.

"Nette, surely we can give her something," said Zeit. "It's not fair . . ."

"I have plenty of pieces with opals in them at home," she replied. "She can pick from one of the pieces I don't wear any longer. And in the meantime, I would like to have this one, Zeit . . ."

In the end, Nette won, as she always seemed to.

For me, it was a Cinderella moment—but not the kind

that little girls dream of. I was dreaming of an exotic, glamorous fairy god-aunt, and instead, I was face-to-face with a full-blown brand of selfishness and meanness I had not fully comprehended before.

My sister was given a plane ticket, time together spent in meaningful ways, and jewelry. I was to get a castoff. Begrudgingly. And only because Zeit had insisted that I get *something*.

The ride back to their house was the kind of quiet that has no description. Zeit tried to break up the tension by giving me a bit of a tour as we drove, but Nette told him that she had a headache and that he should just shut up and get us home.

The house sat high atop a mountain, off a narrow, winding road, at what seemed to me to be the highest point in their town. And there was no fencing to protect me from falling off the mountaintop—what a metaphor for the trip that would be. While it was clear to me that the property, with the mountain views and beautiful green lot, was a multimillion-dollar one, the house itself was shockingly quirky. It seemed to be oddly divided, half of it reflecting Nette and her tastes and half reflecting Zeit and his. It was filled with art from all over the world, arranged with what did not appear to be any thought whatsoever. Computers—at least ten of them, in varying states of repair and functionality—were everywhere, and dance trophies were on every surface that could hold them. Given how elegant my aunt and uncle were in every other respect, their haphazard house brought me great enjoyment. It was as if they weren't nearly as perfect as they looked on the outside.

Once we were there, I was shown to their guest bedroom, which was in the basement, behind the in-home dance studio. Ballroom dance music from a time gone by was playing softly at all times, even when they weren't home. I found it comforting. Finally alone and free to release, I collapsed onto the bed in tears, letting it fully wash over me that this trip had been a horrible mistake. I finally saw things as they actually were. And they were more than ugly. It wasn't just Nette's clear rejection of me that horrified me; it was that I had practically begged for it. I had paid for it. I had forced open a door that was not open to me, and what I found on the other side was a truth I needed to know.

I called my mother to let her know I had arrived safely.

"It's OK so far," I told her. "I don't think Nette and Zeit are getting along right now, so I'm keeping to myself a bit . . ."

I didn't have the words or the energy to share the real story, which I knew would have devastated my mother. Instead, we agreed I should focus on the fact that I would be off to Los Angeles soon. "It's really only one day, sweetheart," she said. "It will go quickly. I know how awful it is when they fight. Call me back if you need me."

The next day at breakfast, Nette presented me with a small yellow-gold ring that had an opal in the center. I did not want it. But I had no choice but to thank her for it and tell her how much I loved it and how generous it was that she was giving it to me. "It's beautiful, Aunt Nette," I said. "Thank you so much for being so generous as to give me one of your rings." The words stuck in my throat. Gracious and painful all at once.

As Nette's fingers were child-sized, the ring did not fit even my pinkie.

"This doesn't fit me," I said. "So I will have to have it sized."

"Of course it doesn't." Her words were clipped. "You're enormous compared to me. We will take it to my jeweler today, and he will take care of it. We don't have anything else to do anyway."

As I contemplated how deftly she had woven in an insult about my appearance and size, I had no choice but to silently remind myself I had asked for all of this. But the final blow came when the jeweler asked if she wanted the charge to be put on her account.

"No," she said. "My niece will pay for it herself."

And so I did.

Later that day, we went back to pick up the ring, and I put it on so Nette could admire it on my hand, which I am quite sure was shaking with the anger I felt. "It's perfect now," I said. "Thank you again."

We had planned to have dinner together that evening, but I lied and said I wasn't feeling well. "I'd like to just try to sleep this headache away," I said. "I hope that is OK . . ."

I escaped to the guest room to count down the hours until I was to be taken to the airport in the morning, quite certain that neither one of us lamented not having dinner together.

It was my first trip to San Francisco, and at that point, I assumed it would be my last. I never wore the ring again. Years later, I told my mother everything, and I gave the ring to a friend who, like me, loved fire opals. I thought perhaps giving it to someone out of love might give the ring and the beautiful stone a new life.

I am grateful to know now, without a shadow of a doubt, that forcing things is not the way. And I still love fire opals, even if I have never quite had the heart to own one.

Chapter Ten

SUMMER CAMP IS A HUGE PART OF JEWISH LIFE. Usually it is sleepaway camp, and it is not unusual for multiple generations to attend the same camp with a great sense of pride. My family's camp is in Oconomowoc, Wisconsin, where my sister and her husband met. Her children were also campers there, and I suspect that my brother, who also went, will send his daughter there someday. After visiting Nette and Zeit, I was on my way to work as the program director at a Jewish overnight camp in Malibu, once again bucking tradition by exploring a camp far from home where I had not ever been a camper.

Once I left San Francisco, I settled into camp life in Malibu and found it was the kind of place that, for me, promoted clarity. Something happens in the mornings there—the sun rises, the fog burns away, and on a clear day, from the right vantage point, you can see forever, including dolphins frol-icking in the ocean. In Malibu, I was able to see Nette and Zeit clearly.

Nette was constantly in attack mode, Zeit constantly in defense mode. But Zeit could not defend me against Nette's viciousness. He would start to defend, to deflect, to try to change the direction of the conversation, but he always folded and gave Nette whatever it was she required in the moment, whether it was material or emotional comfort. I found it hor-rifying and fascinating that my Chinese uncle, who so well knew what it was to be hated for his ethnicity, would allow me to be treated in the same way—in his own house.

I was able to see.

This new clarity should have prepared me for what lay ahead at Alisa and Keith's wedding, which was only a year later. But it didn't. That's the thing. No matter what had come before, I don't think there was any way for me to be truly prepared to hear "Nothing is worse than black."

When a moment like that happens, it is impossible to go back to the way things were. And we did not. It had become something of an odd routine to silently bid farewell to fam-ily members, but none of them had ever behaved so badly in public. Even at my father's funeral, the person who chose to attack me during the service was not someone with whom we had any sort of meaningful relationship. He was not in my life before the funeral, and he was not in it afterward either.

My mother and I have often talked about how different Nette was from the others we've cut out of our lives. For my mother, Nette and her racist betrayal were far more difficult to metabolize than some of the others. It's a bit easier to banish a family member you never really enjoyed in the first place. But my mother loved Nette. Deeply. And for all of the things Nette was, she loved my mother and had always been good to her. My mother's witnessing her outburst inflicted a pain that, to this day, breaks my heart when I think about it. For me, her outburst caused a combination of utter degradation, pain, and embarrassment. But it was also a moment of relief. The truth was, at last, out there.

Still, my mother and I shared a strange kind of heartbreak over Nette's undoing. We both wanted her to be something—someone—she was not able to be.

For years, Nette's behavior had been so elegantly executed as to never be public. She was careful not to be as overtly aggressive as my other relatives had been. It was easy—for both my mother and me—to find other reasons why she treated me differently from my siblings. We probably wanted to. And whenever Nette was confronted, she refused to say anything other than that we were making something out of nothing.

Nette was a master at manipulating people. And she certainly did quite a job when it came to me. Until that day.

For Nette, however, there was also pain. My mother was the closest thing to a daughter that Nette would ever have, and she did not want my mother to see her ugliness, which was usually so carefully masked. When she dropped that mask at Alisa's wedding and my mother saw her naked and unapologetic hatred, Nette's life changed too. In that moment, Nette lost my mother's respect, and that hurt both of them.

We could not go back to the uncomfortable but previously accepted way things had been. And so we didn't. Nette and Zeit did not come back to Chicago after Alisa's wedding.

And life went on.

PART TWO

*Something to remember
when hope gets hard:
Anything is possible
and love is the only
way forward.*

—CLEO WADE

Chapter Eleven

WHEN I SAY THAT LIFE WENT ON, I MEAN THAT I transitioned from the world of musical theater to graduate school to pursue a master's degree in Jewish communal service and then to a career in fundraising. First at the nonprofit level and then in finance. If Nette chose to build her journey through her many marriages, I built mine through what was an oddly organic series of career moves that eventually brought me to film and television production in Los Angeles, where I have happily stayed.

In the summer of 2010, I was ensconced in a life in finance, working with early-stage companies of all sorts. Biotech. Hospitality. Entertainment. Real estate. It was a strange place to land for a girl who could not balance her own checkbook without help. I had made the choice to live part-time in New York and part-time in Chicago, where I would stay with my mother at her house. My work allowed me to travel all over the world, and I did so. First-class flights. Gorgeous hotels. And I travelled for both business and pleasure. From Abu Dhabi to London to Montana to Las Vegas, I had found a way to live and work on my own terms. And I loved it.

But then, an unexpected phone call came.

Fifteen years had passed since my sister's wedding when my mother received a phone call saying that Nette had listed her as her next of kin and that she and Zeit were in rather serious trouble.

In my lifetime, I have eagerly awaited many phone calls. The calls a girl waits for from her current crush. The calls one waits for to find out the plans for the evening. As an actress, I often breathlessly waited by the phone to find out if I had been cast in this show or that one. And I waited by the phone to find out the same when I applied to graduate school. And for jobs.

And then, there are the calls we wait for but don't want to get. The night I waited for my mother to call from the hospital at the end of my father's life was one of the longest of my life. Every time the phone rang, my heart stopped beating. My stomach started to ache. I felt sick.

But what I had never considered was a third kind of call. The unexpected one. Even that call comes in many forms. It's lovely to receive an unexpected call from an old and dear friend with whom you haven't chatted in far too long. Or the call from your brother, sister, nephew, or niece just to say, "I love you," or "I'm thinking of you."

This phone call stood in a class by itself.

"Yes . . . yes . . . I understand," I heard my mother say. Her face grew pale, and I could see her concern grow as she silently nodded, taking in the information being thrown at her.

Nette and Zeit had apparently been conserved by the state of California.

A neighbor had noticed that the house had fallen into disrepair. What had normally been pristine landscaping was overgrown. The mailbox was rarely emptied. Garbage cans had not been taken in after the trash had been collected. Knowing that an elderly couple lived in the house, the neighbor had called Health and Human Services and asked them to do a wellness check.

Clearly, all was not well.

A wellness check meant that someone from the California Department of Aging was dispatched to the house with permission to enter. And when they entered, they found the house overrun with boxes and mail, the kitchen unclean, the whole place a mess. Zeit was apparently quite lucid, but Nette was not. She was, we would come to learn, in the early stages of Alzheimer's, and her memory was touch and go. The state's deputy, having assessed the situation, deemed Nette and Zeit unable to care for themselves, and as they did not have children, the state of California swooped in to become their legal caregivers. This meant that all of the decisions—financial, medical, personal—were being made by someone appointed and approved by the state.

The woman on the phone said my mother was Nette's only living relative. They determined this after reviewing the documents related to Nette's will. She and Zeit had named my mother their mutual executor many years ago and had never changed it.

"As you are Nette's only living relative," the woman told my mother, "we are wondering if you would like to come to California and survey the situation."

My mother remained ashen as she drew a breath. "I'll have to get back to you," she said. "Thank you for the call." She hung up and turned to me with tears in her eyes, quickly telling me everything.

We had not spoken to or seen Nette or Zeit since my sister's wedding. While I knew that my mother never regretted cutting her out of our lives, I also knew that she still held a space for Nette in her heart. Gone is rarely forgotten, and even when a person unflinchingly shows a horrific side of themselves, a soft space remains where love was once present. That made perfect sense to me then, and it makes perfect sense to me now.

Life rarely is black and white.

And so, with this unexpected and shocking phone call came a question: What do we do now?

My family convened to discuss the situation. My brother made it clear that he wanted nothing to do with Nette or the mess in which she found herself. "I will support whatever you decide to do, but I am not going," he said. "This isn't something I feel the need to become involved in." And he meant every word of it.

My sister, with two young children, was not able to travel freely or easily. "I just don't see how I can go there anytime soon . . ." Alisa's voice trailed off. Clearly conflicted but also clear in her choice.

And my mother, who was ill in her own right with a kidney issue, could not go. It was simply not an option.

I was the only person who had yet to speak, and for obvious reasons, I don't think anyone thought I would.

But I found myself questioning. I was able. But was I willing? After everything that had transpired, what was the right thing to do in a circumstance like this? Until this moment, I had never considered what I might do if someone who had been painfully cruel to me needed my help under stressful circumstances. But when I found myself having to decide, the choice was clear. The answers came quickly.

"I'll go," I said. "I'm in L.A. monthly as it is, so I'll just pop up to San Francisco and see what's going on."

My family stared at me blankly.

I will wholly admit I have fantasized in the past about what I would like to do to the many people who have been cruel to me. I have dreamed of what I would say—of what I might do. I have had thousands of pretend confrontational conversations. I have imagined slapping certain people in the face, and as I have never struck another person, that to me is a far more violent act than it might seem to others. I have said things like, "I'll wear a red dress to his funeral one day," or "I'd walk over her bleeding body if it were in front of me." But when I was actually faced with a very real moment when I could have enacted one of my revenge fantasies, I did not.

I defaulted to love.

Please do not mistake me for some sort of sugar-sweet angel. I am far from it. But I believe that before life's traumas obscure it, as so often happens, each of us is born to love and to be loved. I believe that love is why we are here. And this was a test of that belief.

I was San Francisco–bound. And there was no talking me out of it.

"I'll go," I repeated.

The back-and-forth was immediate, for my mother did not want me to be the one who went there. "*You* do not have to do this," she said through teary eyes. "You of all people do not have to do this."

"But it's the right thing to do," I said. "No matter what else has happened, you're all Nette has, and you can't go yourself, so this is the right thing to do. I'll go and see what's going on, and that will be the end of it. I'm sure it will be no big deal."

In spite of her clear hatred for me, Nette had been very good to my mother, and I wanted to give my mother what peace I could around the situation. I chose to go because no matter what else Nette was—or wasn't—to me, I could not imagine simply walking away from a human being in need, much less one who had been something of a surrogate parent to my own beloved mother at one time in her life. My love for my mother in that moment was bigger than anything Nette might have ever said. It really was that simple.

I landed in San Francisco, rented a car, and drove straight to Nette and Zeit's house. I knew from the call my mother had received that Zeit was still living in the house with a caregiver and Nette had been sent to a residential care facility for Alzheimer's patients. But that was really all I knew. I had no game plan other than to go first to the house, then to the Health and Human Services Agency to get a better idea of what was going on, and then to find Nette.

Nette and Zeit still owned the house at the very top of the mountain on Jefferson Avenue. For a city girl like me, used to driving on very flat roads, the drive alone was anxiety-inducing, but that is where this journey began. I had only been there once, but their once pristine and quirky home was clearly now in gross disrepair. And it was heartbreaking. When I walked into the house, I was taken aback. It was silent. No dance music played. Even the television was off. The house looked like it had been ransacked. There were boxes, some empty and some full, all over the house. Garbage filled the kitchen. On the formerly immaculate countertops. In the sink. Laundry, unfolded, was heaped in several baskets. Even with Zeit's caregiver present, it was clear that only the barest minimum of care was being given. The house smelled. Stale. Old. And like pain.

Zeit was sleeping in his easy chair, and his caregiver was puttering around in the kitchen. The caregiver pulled me outside, and we exchanged basic but uncomfortable pleasantries.

"I'm Nette and Zeit's great-niece," I explained, "and I'm here to see what is going on with them. Can you please give me an update on Zeit's health?"

"*You* are their niece?" As always, incredulity followed any mention of me being family.

"I am," I replied, "and I'd like to have a full download on Zeit's condition and plan for care. Please."

"Can you provide any proof of your relationship?"

Annoyed, uncomfortable, and horrified by the condition in which I had found both Zeit and the house, I handed the caregiver a notarized letter verifying my identity. My mother had insisted I bring it. As ever, she was right.

The caregiver gave me an overview: Even now, in his early nineties, Zeit was well enough in mind, but his body was steadily failing. His sadness from being separated from Nette was only making his decline more rapid. Zeit did not want to leave the house for a care facility, and so the state decided to try things this way.

I went back inside to check on my uncle. "How are you feeling, Uncle Zeit?" I leaned down to kiss his cheek and to get the story straight from him.

"How do you think I am?" he said. He started to weep. He told me about how state officials had come into the house and taken Nette from him. About how they had taken away his money. His telephone. His freedom. His dignity.

"I'm here now, and I'm going to see what I can do to make things better," I said. "I promise. I'm going to visit Nette, and then I'll come back and see you again. Very soon."

I could not wait to leave. My chest was tight. My heart hurt. And the tears were coming—fast and furious, like Zeit's rant.

Tomorrow would be another day. And I needed to get some rest.

For some reason that remains a mystery to this day, I was not allowed to have the address for Nette's facility until I paid a visit to the Senior Services office that had conserved her in the first place. It took at least five phone calls to actually get someone on the line; my many messages were not returned. And once I finally received a return call, I found that the office itself was in a repurposed middle school. It had clearly not been redecorated in at least forty years and was almost as depressing as Nette and Zeit's house.

The tiny office was like something out of an episode of *Law & Order*. There was a desk overflowing with files and a visibly overworked administrator who greeted me. I had my identity letter at the ready. And, of course, I had to use it. The administrator gave an overview of how Nette ended up in the facility, but I had far more questions than she had answers, the logical byproduct of the fifteen-year estrangement between my aunt and me.

"Can you please help me to understand the process?" I began. "How was the decision made to conserve them? And how did you choose Nette's facility?"

The administrator stopped me.

"Young lady, I have a few questions of my own," she snapped. The judgment in her eyes was obvious. She asked me one question. "How did your mother . . . your family allow this to happen?"

I could tell from her tone that sharing even a small part of my story—our story—would not be well received, much less understood. And I did not think it would help my case. For even without seeing Nette, I had already decided I was going to do everything in my power to move her to a facility in Chicago to be near my mother and sister.

I told the administrator, simply, that we were not particularly close because of the distance, and we moved on. At long last, I was given the address for Nette's care facility. I was also given contact information for a conservator the state had assigned. She was charged with managing Nette's and Zeit's care and finances, and she would be the contact person for anything related to them from here forward.

It took a bit of doing to find Nette's facility, and when I finally did manage to find it, I saw that it was more a ramshackle home than anything else. I learned quickly that California was filled with care facilities that were actually *homes*—houses tucked away in residential neighborhoods and retrofitted to accommodate six to eight patients each. This was one of those places, and it was, in a word, bleak.

The outside of the home was in desperate need of paint and a lawn care service, and the inside wasn't much better. The halls were dark, and the yellow-beige paint on the walls was cracked. The floors were tiled with cheap linoleum. And the stench of industrial-level cleaners was nauseating. At least, I thought, it was clean. Or at least it smelled like it was. There was minimal security, and I was able to walk in without anyone asking me who I was or what I was doing there.

I managed to hunt down someone who said she was a nurse. As she was not wearing a uniform, I couldn't be sure. That day, I really wasn't sure of much. "I'm here to see Nette CeKansky Wang," I told her. "I am her niece."

Once again, incredulous eyes looked me up and down.

"I have a letter. Here." It had taken only a few of these

exchanges for me to grow tired of justifying myself, and the letter quickly became both my introduction and my shield.

"This way," the nurse said. Truthfully, I'm not sure that she was really a medical professional. Absent any sort of uniform or name tag, I had no way of knowing who she was or what her qualifications were. And I definitely wanted to know. My initial research made it clear that Alzheimer's and dementia care is very specific, and I wanted to be sure that Nette was being cared for by people who knew what they were doing. I added that to my growing list of questions for the administrator and the conservator.

She led me down a dark, narrow hallway that was—at least in my mind—much longer than it should have been. I stood in Nette's doorway surveying the room, which was also dark and narrow. Nette was sitting up in a small bed, covered in a blanket. It took her all of thirty seconds to see me standing there. Even with Alzheimer's now officially diagnosed, she was lucid that day and true to the Nette I had always known, her filter fully disengaged. Secretly, I might have hoped to find her otherwise.

"They sent *you?*" she said. "As if being trapped in this place isn't bad enough, they had to send you."

Nette's situation was not pretty. Her hair had not been brushed, much less styled. Her nails were bare—something I had never seen in all the years I had known her. Not a drop of makeup adorned her face, and when I dared to get a bit closer to her, I saw dried food on her shirt and in the corners of her mouth. She was a mess. In spite of her unkempt state, she retained her familiar and remarkable combination of outrage and dignity as she stared me down.

It was not the welcome I was hoping for, but it was authentic, and Nette was nothing if not authentic. But this time, I was not silent. I did not shrink. This time, we were alone. There was no wedding. I had no reason not to make a scene. And so I fired back at her.

"Yes," I said. "They sent me. And I'm your only option. So choose. Stay here forever, or deal with me and I'll try to get you out of here."

"Fine," she said.

It seemed there was something worse than black for Nette after all, and that was the thought of having to live out the rest of her days in what amounted to a one-star hotel. Her own potential salvation far outweighed her disdain for me and my blackness. Her choice was as immediate as mine had been to come in the first place, although we clearly had made our choices from much different places.

The visit lasted all of twenty minutes. It was all that either one of us could take. I drove back to the hotel crying. I'm not even sure why. Maybe it was from the sheer stress of it all. Maybe it was because the "home" Nette was in was far from acceptable. Maybe it was because I knew I had just bitten off far more than I might be able to chew.

Chapter Twelve

WHEN I RETURNED TO CHICAGO, I TOLD MY MOTHER what I had learned. What I had seen. And I told her about my not-at-all-formed plan to bring Nette to Chicago.

"If it won't be too much for you, and you feel like that is the thing to do, then we should do it," said my mother. "But only if it won't be too much for you. Or hurt you. You are the most important thing."

"I'll be just fine, Mama," I said. "This is the right thing to do."

As I was already in the routine of going to Los Angeles monthly for business, it made sense for me to tack on a few days in San Francisco each month while I was, essentially, in the neighborhood. I would visit Zeit, visit Nette, and somehow figure out how to get her sent to a care facility in Chicago. I mean, how hard could it be?

What is it that they say? "Be careful what you wish for"? Or "No good deed goes unpunished"?

I knew nothing about how to manage this kind of situation or about what I came to understand were the strict California laws designed to protect the elderly. And I do mean nothing. But knowing nothing had never prevented me from diving headfirst into a situation, and it did not stop me now.

On my next trip, I knew enough to go straight to the hotel to get myself grounded before embarking on any visits. I checked myself in to the Four Seasons at Palo Alto for a night of rest before digging in the next day. The Four Seasons would become my de facto home on every trip I would eventually take, and for me, a lovely meal, a hot bath, and a good scotch were essential to getting anything done.

The next morning, I set off to meet Paula. The conservator.

At first, I was hopeful that the conservator would be my partner in getting Nette and Zeit's situation sorted out. God knows I needed someone who understood the system to help me understand it. I assumed she would want to release them to the care of their families. The state hadn't known that we existed before, but now it did, and surely the conservator would be relieved to know that Nette and Zeit did have family to look after them. I assumed she would want them to live out their days in the manner to which they had grown accustomed: in comfort, elegance, and grace.

I could not have been more wrong.

We met at a coffee shop in Redwood City, close to the house but far enough away for Zeit not to be privy to the conversation. At barely five feet tall, Paula was small. Both in stature and in character, I would soon come to find. She was in her midfifties and was bespectacled, and she definitely seemed to have an overcompensation thing going on.

"Nice to meet you," I said. "I'm Marra, Nette and Zeit's great-niece. My mother is Nette's niece and the executor of both of their trusts and wills. As she is unable to travel, I am acting as her proxy."

Paula eyed me with some suspicion. "But I thought Nette was Jewish," she said. "I am Jewish."

"I am too. And I *am* her great-niece."

"Well," she said, "I am the daughter that seniors like Nette and Zeit never had—and sorely need."

And she was serious. Paula was not accustomed to having a family member participate in her affairs because most of her clients did not have family that would or could participate. In many cases, she ended up working with elderly people who did not have children or any relatives, and so she was given free rein to make decisions. And when I say "free rein," I do mean completely unfettered and unmonitored access to money, real estate, and personal property. The state, through some sort of "certification" process, had a number of these conservators. And to this day, I have never been able to determine exactly what the certification process entails.

"Well, Nette and Zeit may not have had children," I said, "but they do have us. And I'm here to make sure we are working together to ensure that their final days are as they should be."

That Paula had to include anyone in her efforts was an unwelcome surprise for her. That she had to include a type A person who expected to be present for every single conversation was an even more unwelcome one. She was not shy about her feelings. I knew the moment she held up her hand in front of my face to stop me from speaking that we were not on the same page. And that we had very different ideas about how to work respectfully together. There is nothing I loathe more than to have someone push their hand in my face.

I have always been a questioner. My mother says that from the moment I had enough words, I would constantly ask, "But . . . *why?*" I wanted to know why the sky would turn different colors and why I could not read another book. I wanted to know why I had to try foods that did not interest me. Why my sister wanted to play with my toys. I wanted to know the why of every single thing.

When I was a child, Rabbi Schaalman taught us that our questions were essential. As I grew older, in Hebrew school, my questions were encouraged. And so, at least at the synagogue, I was free to ask them, even if my teachers in day school did not always welcome them.

When I attended a Catholic high school, the nuns loathed

my desire to know why. On my very first day, during my very first religion class, I wanted to know why they believed in the Immaculate Conception. The poor nun, Sister V, who had been charged with teaching my class, did not want to answer me, and she was ill-equipped to deal with the persistence that my parents and Rabbi Schaalman had taught me was my birthright.

"But, Sister," I said, "I don't understand why you think Mary was a virgin. She had a husband. And don't husbands and wives have sex? And why do you kneel and pray to a statue of her? Isn't that idolatry? And that's against the Ten Commandments . . ."

"Miss Gad, that is *enough*!" Sister V was incensed that I dared to question the belief in the Virgin Mary. That I also dared to mention sex in class was a bridge too far. "You may excuse yourself and go to the dean's office. Perhaps she will help you to better understand how things are done here and that there are appropriate and inappropriate questions that one can ask."

The dean was a bit gentler than Sister V, but the message was the same. "We don't encourage questions about the core of our religion here," she told me. "Perhaps your rabbi would be a better resource for you."

"But don't you know more than he does about your religion?" I asked.

I very quickly realized that Paula appreciated my questions as much as the nuns had. I think I have always been a question-focused being because I want to understand the process. And when it came to Nette's conservation, I understood nothing; therefore, I had more questions than answers.

On a macro level, I wanted to know what to expect from the process of moving Nette from the state's custody to ours. Once the state decided to intervene and declared Nette mentally unfit to make her own decisions, all of her care and the decisions around her body, finances, and soul fell under the state's control. And therefore, Paula's. I had already decided it would be best to put Nette into my mother's custody and then move her to a facility in Illinois. That way, my mother and sister would be able to care for her. I needed to understand what the legal processes would be, how long I should expect things to take, what would be expected of me, if I needed an attorney . . .

And those questions were just the initial ones.

"I'd like to start with my hopeful endgame and work backward from there," I told Paula. "As my mother is Nette's closest living relative and she is in Chicago, we would like to begin the process of transferring Nette to a facility there." I pulled out my list of questions and thought it made sense to get down to business.

"You seem to think you're in charge of this process. Clearly you don't understand how this works," Paula sneered.

"Perhaps I don't," I said. "Why don't you enlighten me? Starting with your job description."

I bit back. In retrospect, that was probably not the smartest move. But I was tired and overwhelmed and not in the mood for her nastiness when we should have been on the same page.

Once Paula laid out the basics of her job, I moved on to ask for an accounting of what she had done to date, including money she had spent—and then I wanted to come up with an action plan for the future. Like I said: I am type A and I take charge.

Normally, this worked well. I have always held jobs that allowed me to flex my natural leadership. Come on—I produce film and television for a living. Getting to the desired finish line and sorting out where to move next when the playing field gets challenging is how I spend my days. But this time, it turned out, I couldn't take charge. Paula was in charge of everything. And while she did have an obligation to include me, it was at her discretion.

So when I asked her why there had been no progress made toward finding realtors to sell Nette and Zeit's house, she simply didn't answer me. When I asked why she was being paid to make weekly visits to Nette in her care facility but, according to the facility manager, had gone only twice in many months, she again didn't answer.

She didn't have to.

"Young lady, you are going to have to trust me," she said. "I have been doing this for many years, and I know what is best. Period."

It was the first of many standoffs, and I clearly was not the victor.

We then went to the house to survey Nette's and Zeit's belongings and to see Zeit. Zeit turned away from Paula when she walked in, but he smiled at me and accepted my kiss on his cheek. As had happened the last time, he began to weep about how "they" had taken everything from him. Paula, hearing this, became enraged.

"We are doing what is best for you," she told Zeit sharply, "and that is the end of it."

No compassion. No empathy. No humanity.

"What do you need, Uncle Zeit?" I asked. "Would you like some magazines? A book, perhaps?"

"I want to see Nette," he said. "They won't let me see her, and I don't know why. They won't even tell me where she is. And I want my computers back. That would be so nice."

Zeit had always had a healthy obsession with computers, fueled, I suspect, by his background as an engineer for Lockheed. And in his later years, he had taken to purchasing them, taking them apart, and trying to re-engineer them into something better. That he had no access whatsoever to Nette was bad enough. That his computers had been taken away was too much for him to bear. They were his raison d'être, and without them, he sat. Doing nothing.

And so, for the second standoff of the day, I demanded that Paula allow Zeit to tinker with his computers. I could not understand why Zeit would be denied that pleasure and the distraction of it. We would get into the Nette-related issues privately, out of Zeit's earshot. When Paula again opened her mouth to refuse, I cut her off, saying, "I'm sure that you want him to be happy. Don't you?"

The question silenced her, and she relented. Zeit could have his computers. And I had a small victory.

We then went to Nette's bedroom to gather a few things before heading off to visit her. Now that I had seen her room at the facility and her nearly empty closet there, I wanted to bring some of her clothes and a few photos to make the space a bit more palatable. "I don't know what you think she needs," Paula said as we reached Nette's room. "I've already made sure she has clothing. We should just go."

I opened the door and found that her once pristine bedroom looked as if it had been ransacked, with drawers open and things strewn about the room and floor. Apparently, Paula had packed up Nette's gorgeous wardrobe, leaving only what she deemed necessary for her to wear. All of her beautiful pantsuits were in bags, heaped upon one another. Her shoes, easily one hundred pairs, were piled in a corner. Later, I would find her ball gowns crammed onto a rack in the filthy garage. I did not know where to find anything in the mess, so I gathered a few photographs of the family to place in her room and we set off.

She was out of her bed when we arrived, and I was able to see her much more clearly than I had the first time I visited.

"What is she *wearing*?" I exclaimed.

Paula's idea of clothing meant ill-fitting sweat suits she purchased at Walmart. I was horrified. Nette was wearing a sweatshirt that was two sizes too big and emblazoned with a glittery cat. Nette did like to sparkle. But not this way. And she definitely did not like cats.

"There is absolutely no reason for her to be decked out in the outlandish costumes I found in her closet."

"But those are her clothes!" I said. "Doesn't she have the right to wear her own clothing? It won't cost the state anything!" I looked Nette over again and added, "Presuming you actually spent money on this hideous ensemble. What a waste!"

Paula fell silent.

To make matters worse, she had stopped Nette's hair and nail appointments, and so my once always perfectly coiffed aunt was left completely unkempt. Her nails were broken and unpolished. Her hair had not been washed in so long that it was greasy, and whoever had been washing her hair was not using her lavender shampoo that left her white hair silver and beautiful. It was yellow. She had chin hairs sprouting everywhere. She was a disaster. Even in her state of diminished capacity, I couldn't imagine that her appearance didn't bother her. At least a bit.

I thought I would start at the top, with her hair, and work my way down. I found her hairbrush and came to her side, trying in vain to brush her greasy, limp hair. Nette flinched and grumbled each time I touched her.

"Do you really have to touch me? Why are you touching me?"

"How about a manicure, Aunt Nette?" I couldn't stand to see her this way. And in a situation that was starting to feel just a bit out of my control, trying to get her a bit tidier felt like something I could accomplish. "Or I can get tweezers and clean up your chin?" I tried to hold up a hand mirror to her face so she might see what I was talking about, but she pushed my hand and the mirror away.

There we were. Paula glowering. Nette grumbling. And me. Trying not to lose my cool with both of them.

"I don't need to see my face," Nette said. "I know my own face. And I don't need you to touch me!"

"This really isn't necessary," Paula mumbled under her breath.

"Yes," I replied. "It is. It is essential. Nette has always been an elegant, well-kept woman, and there is absolutely no reason for her to go from looking like Zsa Zsa Gabor to looking like Eliza Doolittle at the start of *My Fair Lady*."

I was insistent. And even with frustrated tears starting to well up in my eyes and my chest starting to hurt from the stress of it all, I continued to try to do what little I could to restore Nette to her former state of elegance, even if she was in a cat-emblazoned sweatshirt.

I now knew that Paula, Zeit and Nette's "daughter" of a conservator, was criminal in her neglect. I will never understand the indignity and madness of it all. Nette and Zeit had plenty of money in the bank, and that money should have ensured that the rest of their days would be lived out at the same level of quality they had enjoyed before they were separated. And before they were declared incompetent. I also understood that Paula and I were not likely to see eye to eye on anything. As she was in charge, I would have to proceed carefully if I was to have any success at all in my endeavors.

Paula's default position was that I should "trust her" to do her job. And once I realized she was not going to answer my very reasonable questions, I knew I could not trust her. She refused to account for how she billed my aunt's estate for her time. She refused to explain why valuable things like furs and jewelry seemed to be absent from my aunt's closets. She questioned my every move, even though I paid all of my own expenses, and she wanted to know why I insisted upon attending each court date and why, in spite of what was clearly a tense relationship, I insisted upon seeing my aunt once per month.

Unfortunately, she was also in charge of Zeit's estate. While my mother had a bit of standing there in that she would ultimately be the executor of both Nette's and Zeit's wills, there was nothing I could do to intervene on Zeit's behalf. And it was devastating.

It was one thing to see two people, once the very definition of vibrancy, fade into a version of infirm old age that is the stuff of horror dramas. It was quite another to be almost helpless in trying to make sure their final years were in keeping with the lives—and estates—they had earned. I was forced to stand by and witness what amounted to criminal theft: Nette's and Zeit's estates were picked clean by their state-appointed "daughter," who did not have to account for anything.

Sadly, it was a crime for which there seemed no recourse.

It turned out that I did need to have an attorney on hand and that there are attorneys who specialize in cases like ours. As mine had been referred to me by someone other than the dreadful Paula, I felt free to share with him my concerns about Paula's behavior and her unwillingness to answer basic questions.

"Surely there is some sort of reporting process," I said. "Isn't there? There has to be a board or something to which she must be held accountable."

"You're best served not to do that," said my attorney. "This is a very small community, and she would certainly find out that you were the one who filed the report. Remember that she has the power to punish Nette and Zeit—and you. While your plan to move Nette is perfectly reasonable and should be allowed, Paula can keep her here in California if that is what she wants to do. And that isn't what you want. Let's just get through it and leave her alone."

"But that seems so unfair," I said. "This all seems patently unfair. To all of us."

"That may be true. But that is where we are. And this is going to be a marathon. Not a sprint. You should plan on the process with the courts to take a number of months. Perhaps longer than a year."

"I didn't realize it would be so onerous," I replied.

"Oh, yes," said my attorney. "And remember, even if you can get Paula and the judge to agree to move Nette, Paula will likely retain control over the money, so you'll have to deal with her for as long as Nette and Zeit are alive."

Impotence is not a state of mind I had ever experienced until this moment. And it was excruciating.

But upon the advice of my counsel, I did my best to be polite and to limit my questions, neither of which I wanted to do. This did nothing to create comfort with Paula, as she already knew I was suspicious of her work. But I knew it was my only move if I wanted to succeed.

This may have been the first and only time in my life that I felt knowledge is not power, for I was powerless on almost every possible front. And it felt as awful as everything else that was going on.

Chapter Thirteen

EVENTUALLY, A RHYTHM SET IN AND I WAS GOING TO San Francisco on a monthly basis to spend time with Nette, Zeit, and the charming Paula. As I had started to focus my career on film finance, I was already in the rhythm of travelling to Los Angeles each month. The old-fashioned girl in me has always believed that doing business face-to-face is best, and those early trips allowed me to build a base of colleagues and friends I hold to this day.

The routine was almost always the same. I would fly from Los Angeles to San Jose, rent a car, and go directly to the hotel. While many people dream of staying regularly at a Four Seasons, few would want to be there for the reason that I was. But the hotel became my safe place, where I knew that everything was beautiful and I would be well cared for. The staff came to know me well, and they knew why I was coming each month. They grew accustomed to seeing me pull up after a visit with Nette, either still crying behind my large, black sunglasses or so tear-stained that it was obvious I had been crying. There was always a gentle pat on my shoulder from the doorman as I passed through and headed up to my room.

And there were always scotch and chocolate in my room from the management.

Of course, the business of my career still had to be managed during these trips, and I would often find myself having to take phone calls from investors or clients between visits and meetings with Nette, Zeit, Paula, and the court. My theater background came in handy during these moments, for I was able to pull myself together—and perform—no matter what the circumstance. During my theater days, when I was doing a fifteen-week run of *Little Shop of Horrors*, I was once so sick that I passed out during the show. But I didn't pass out onstage. I waited until intermission. This was no different.

I always let Paula know I was coming one week prior so that we might find a time for both of us to meet either at the house, where Zeit still lived, or at Nette's care facility. Without fail, I would receive back a note saying that it was a "rough" or "busy" time for her but that she would do her best to find time for me. What she spent so much time doing, I will never know, but I am certain it was not caring for Nette and Zeit.

My visits were not longer than two full days unless we had to go to court. On the first day, I would visit Zeit and see what progress had been made in preparing the house to be sold. Always, it seemed, I would find both the house and Zeit in a steady state of decline.

I never saw Zeit move. I never saw him anywhere other than seated in a recliner in the living room, with his feet up. Wrapped in a blanket, no matter how warm the weather might be. The room, like the rest of the house, was overflowing with boxes that never seemed to be emptied or filled. It was like stepping into the very definition of inaction. And it was depressing. His "caregiver" was in the house, but he wasn't really there, as he was never in the room with Zeit. He was puttering around either outside or in the kitchen. Usually on the phone. But never did I see him interact with Zeit.

"How are you feeling, Uncle Zeit?" I would ask. Just the question brought tears.

"I am tired," he would cry. "They have taken everything away from me. I cannot make any decisions for myself. They won't let me see Nette. They won't let me talk to Nette. They won't let me do anything. I wish this would all be over."

To try to comfort a crying child is a challenge. But to try to comfort a nonagenarian who had once been elegant, commanding, and vibrant is devastating and virtually impossible.

If Paula was with me, she would often try to intervene,

saying things like, "You know that this is all in your best interest, Mr. Wang. We all just want what is best for you."

"I *know* what is best for me," Zeit would snap back. And Paula would then leave the room, presumably to pretend to pack up a box out of earshot.

"I wish I could make this better for you," I would say, "that I could bring you to see Nette, but she is sick, Uncle Zeit. That is why you can't see her right now. We don't want you to get sick too."

We both knew it was a lie and that Nette's illness was not contagious. But it seemed the most compassionate thing to tell him. And so I told the lie each time I saw him. And he let me.

I always started with a chat with his caregiver to get a sense of how his health was, and the answer was almost uniformly the same.

"His mind is fine. His body is failing. He's old. This is what happens."

I have never seen someone less interested in trying to make sure that every drop was being drunk out of the cup of life than was Zeit's caregiver. It was almost as if both he and Zeit were simply waiting for Zeit to die.

I would then move on to Paula, trying to get what information she would give about the preparation of the house for sale.

"We really do need to get the house put on the market, Paula," I would say. "Can you please give a sense of when you will complete your inventory of Nette's and Zeit's belongings? And where you will store them? And which real estate agents you have spoken with about the value of the house?"

"I am doing the best I can," she would reply. "You don't understand what a big job this is." Paula always had an excuse, even if she was being paid by the hour out of this very estate.

"I'm happy to help," I would offer. "I can come up and help pack boxes. Or I can call real estate agents so that we can start to get a sense of the value of the property. Just let me know what I can do."

"You can let me do my job. That would be helpful."

"And you can actually do your job," I would think to myself. In my outside voice, it was always, "Thank you, Paula. We appreciate all of your efforts."

Then I would say goodbye to Zeit. "I'll be back in a few weeks, Uncle Zeit," I would say. "Take good care . . ."

And after planting a kiss on Zeit's damp and wrinkled cheek, I would leave. I tried to never let Zeit see me cry.

Anyone who knows me knows I am a big believer in therapy. I think it is the greatest gift one can consistently give to oneself. And as an act of self-love, it truly has been both life-saving and transformative for me. I often joke with my siblings that I'm going to give them a therapist as a birthday gift. Not surprisingly, they've never taken me up on it!

One of the things I have learned about myself through twenty-five years of therapy is that I created a system of defenses designed to insulate me from the many places where I felt I was constantly under attack. I insulated myself inside of my own body by gaining weight. And my emotional defenses meant living in a state where I was constantly bracing myself for the next horrible thing to happen.

I was waiting for the next racist comment to be spoken.

For the next person to tell me that I was not acceptable.

That I was an abomination in the eyes of God. (That was always a favorite.)

That I was "unusual-looking."

I was constantly waiting for the other shoe to drop. If an animal has been abused repeatedly, its expectation is never that its owner will be loving and kind. Its expectation is that there will be another beating.

That was certainly the case for me with Nette. And during these monthly visits, my defenses, built over years, were on high alert.

I usually went to see Nette on the second day of my visit, and gearing myself up was a process all its own. I have meditated daily for more than twenty years, but on the days I knew I would be visiting Nette, I would meditate twice, hoping fervently that the peace meditation brings me might double. Knowing how particular Nette has always been about appearances, I would dress carefully. I made sure my hair and makeup were at their best so that there was no space for her to comment. Not that it ever stopped her, but in my mind, looking good and feeling good have always been intertwined, and every little bit would help. I was, as is my way, trying to set myself up for success.

Then I would get into the car.

Usually a lover of music and perpetually giving a car concert, I would instead silently drive to her facility, trying to visualize a pleasant exchange between us rather than relive every ugly greeting I had ever received. The drive usually took about twenty minutes. Sometimes I actually talked to myself aloud, hoping it might mean I would hear myself better.

Then, as I pulled up, I would look in the rearview mirror and give myself a pep talk. "You can do this, Marra," I would say aloud. "You can do anything. An hour with Nette is going to be a piece of cake." The irony of that turn of phrase was not lost on me, given how often Nette criticized me for my weight—and how much she secretly had always loved cake herself.

The visits always began in the same way—with some version of an unpleasant comment, an eye roll. A combination of passive and aggressive as only Nette could be. And they often ended in similar fashion.

"It's you," Nette always said. "Again." Sometimes the tone was angry. Sometimes it was annoyed. But the words were almost always the same.

"Yes, it's me," I would say. "I've come to check on you and to see how you're feeling. How are you feeling?"

"With my hands. How do you feel?" What had always been a joke told by my dear uncle Harold, accompanied by an affectionate tousle of my hair, was biting sarcasm coming out of her tiny, thin mouth. Although Nette by then had what was considered advancing Alzheimer's, she was fairly lucid—at least when it came to remembering me.

I would then try to get close enough to do my version of a wellness check. To find Nette in fresh clothing and with her hair clean became something of a victory. And that victory only came after I had carefully let Paula know that these things were critically important.

After looking her over, I would spend some time checking in with Nette's caregivers, asking about her progress and moods and really just cooling off.

"How are her visits with Paula going?" I would ask.

"She really doesn't come very much. Maybe she comes once every four or five weeks. And she comes for a few minutes, looks at her, asks if there have been any changes, and then she leaves."

As much as I love being right, I hated being so right about this.

Finally, I would take Nette to the TV room, where I could defuse her nastiness by trying to chat with the other residents. During my limited interactions with them, they never seemed to have visitors, and they welcomed conversation of any kind.

Unlike my aunt, they were thrilled to see me. Always. It is heartbreaking to see people left alone to slip into the darkness of Alzheimer's. Perhaps their families could not bear to watch them deteriorate. Perhaps they didn't have families. In any case, seeing the other residents sitting alone was always what propelled me to try to engage with Nette.

"Is there anything special I can bring for you the next time I come?" I would ask. "Hopefully, we will be bringing you to Chicago so that you can be closer to my mom very soon. Are you sure you don't want anything?"

Typically, my questions were met with silence.

I would try to file her nails or brush her hair. My touch always caused her to recoil, as if I were burning her skin. The dance, at least, had become familiar.

"Do not *touch* me!"

I was always amazed that no one ever came running down the long, narrow hallway to see what might be going on. To see why Nette was shouting. If I might need some assistance. But no one ever came. There seemed to be little interest in saving either one of us.

No matter how complicated and ugly our relationship was, I was there. And I was doing my best. Whatever that meant for the day. When I could take no more, I would leave. In spite of my meticulous preparation and double meditation routine, I found that I could handle visiting with Nette for an average of only forty-five minutes at a time. And really, I wanted to leave after about fifteen minutes.

The ride back to the hotel was similar to the ride to the care facility. It was made in silence. But the ride back was always driven through a veil of tears. They always came. I tried to tell myself that she didn't deserve my tears, but really, I wasn't crying for her. I was crying for myself. And the sheer madness of the situation in which I had willingly, and somehow not at all regretfully, put myself.

Chapter Fourteen

It took only a few months for an unfortunate sense of routine to take hold during my monthly visits to San Francisco. My time with Zeit was always sad because he was so sad. So broken. And so aware of all of it.

My time with Paula was profoundly frustrating because I was forced to swallow every word I truly wanted to speak, forced to bite my tongue until it was raw, and forced to allow her to control the process. My time with Nette was like badly prepared icing on an ill-made cake. It was simply unpalatable.

During one visit, Nette was especially agitated. She could not sit still and was constantly shifting in search of a comfortable spot. On a good day, I could do nothing right. But on this day, I was simply . . . wrong.

"It's just not right that I have to have you handling everything," she said. "Where is your mother?"

"As I've told you, Nette, she is sick," I said. "She has a rather serious kidney issue, and she cannot travel back and forth. I am the only option."

"Do you even know how to do things right?"

"I am a genius. Remember? In the literal sense?" Insulting my intelligence was a new thing. Even for her. And it was not something I was willing to take lightly. "I'm quite sure I can figure out how to manage you and your care. And if you want me to continue, I'll thank you to stop insulting me."

"At least be sure to close the door all the way when you go."

I gladly closed the door. Loudly. And I left. For both of us, it was definitely time for me to go.

The next month, I put on my figurative armor, gearing myself up for a visit that would be as bad as, if not worse than, the last. It had been, after all, an endless stream of contentious, stressful visits. I had no reason to think four weeks would change anything for the better.

I took the long walk down the dark, narrow hallway and opened the door.

"Who are you, pretty lady?"

I was greeted by a docile, sweet voice. For a moment, I thought I might be trying to enter the wrong room. Then I looked around to see whom Nette was actually speaking to because I was positively sure she was not speaking to me. I guess I had forgotten that she had Alzheimer's. I had forgotten that, at some point, the disease would do deeper work and change her. And that the routine would then change. I had heard that it happens in an instant. That one moment someone is "there" and in the next moment they are gone. And that is exactly how it happened.

"Who are you, pretty lady?" Nette asked again.

Still, I stood there. Silent. Dumbfounded.

I did not know how to respond.

When I was a young girl and teenager, I wanted to be pretty. No—I wanted to be told I was pretty. Instead, I was routinely told I was smart.

"You're so brilliant," people would say.

"You're so creative."

But no one really told me I was pretty.

What I really wanted was for certain people to think I was pretty. And for the longest time, Nette was at the top of that list. Given what I considered to be her maximum level of glamour and style at all times, to be deemed pretty by her was my dream. I gave that up, of course, the moment she told me that nothing was worse than my very existence.

I moved closer to make sure she could see me, and I simply said, "It's Marra." I waited for the Nette I knew to roar out of her tiny mouth. "How are you feeling today, Aunt Nette?"

Nette didn't answer immediately. Instead, she smiled a smile as sweet as her voice. After a few moments that felt like an hour, she spoke again.

"I'm feeling fine. Why are you here today?"

Again, I was struck silent, paralyzed in a new land where Nette did not know me, where I was a "pretty lady." And where I no longer knew her.

You really are very pretty.

She had said it once before—on Alisa's wedding day. But that was a different Nette, with a very different voice. That time, it was a sneer. Not a compliment. And it did not feel good to be on the receiving end of it. In that moment, I started to shift my understanding of external validation; her comments taught me well that it is far more important for me to define and own who and what I am than to allow that to be dictated by the praise or vitriol of others.

Nevertheless, to hear genuine words of kindness—a compliment, no less—come out of a mouth that had hurled pure racist hatred was stunning. And a bit scary, for I was not sure in that moment if it was real. Or true.

The only thing I knew was that it was different now. Nette was different. That's the thing about Alzheimer's. You never know when your person will change. Or how. You only know that once it happens, nothing will ever be the same again.

Anyone dealing with someone with Alzheimer's knows of the transformation that takes place. So often, people with a loved one living with Alzheimer's talk about how the disease turns that loved one into a horrible stranger. A person who was once loving and kind might become angry. Vulgar.

Violent. The disease brings out the darker, uglier sides of our humanity, thereby making an already heartbreaking decline all the more so. I cannot imagine the pain of watching someone who was once gentle and nurturing become different. And I've read many stories about how powerfully sad it is the first time the eyes looking back at you don't recognize you at all.

But in my upside-down world, Alzheimer's turned an abusive, mean woman into someone docile. Sweet. Complimentary. And the eyes that no longer recognized me no longer saw me as ugly or inferior. The disease turned Nette into someone I had always hoped she was. Because of the way I experienced it in Nette, I have often wondered if Alzheimer's and dementia simply bring people back to who they are on the inside, before the world changed them. Perhaps, like the disease itself, each stripping away of memory and persona is different. Perhaps this was the universe's strange gift to me. A way of letting me see that there was a loving being inside her angry shell. I took it as a validation of a theory I have always held: that we are all born as loving beings. Eventually, some people let life bury that love inside of an angry, mean exterior.

I'll never really know why it happened this way. Years later, I find myself still wondering why.

Chapter Fifteen

No matter what else I might say about Nette, I do believe that she lived in search of love and romance, and that in the end, she found the best love of her life in Zeit. Of her many husbands, he was the one she was married to longest—and that union lasted for nearly forty years.

Theirs was, to say the least, an unconventional marriage. But I like to think that much like the people who were in it, it was authentic and honest in a way that many marriages are not. Even when it was—perhaps mostly when it was—at its most uncomfortable.

Nette nodded to it herself at my sister's wedding. That she, as a white, Jewish woman, had elected to take a Chinese husband during the 1960s was considered, at best, scandalous. At worst, it was viewed through the same ugly, racist eyes that had proclaimed my beautiful family an abomination. Either way, it was not warmly embraced.

They were childless. They travelled the world extensively and tirelessly. They were champion ballroom dancers. Nette absolutely had attachments, emotional and sexual, to other men, which Zeit knew about and, on some level, supported.

For them, it worked, even when they were screaming at each other, hurling insults that would certainly belie the idea that love existed between the two of them. It worked. And in a society that can draw "successful" marriages at times in two-dimensional, almost cartoonish terms—always including romantic proposals, white weddings, monogamy, and some level of approval of the match and lifestyle from family and friends—Nette and Zeit defied all of the norms. And they did so without apology.

In many ways, the authenticity of their union inspires me today as I search for something that authentically works for me and my eventual partner. While I don't wish to have the level of conflict that seemed to be an everyday energy in Nette and Zeit's marriage, I do want to have a relationship that is about my partner and me—and not about what everyone else believes is the "right" way to do things. I've known only one man willing to delve into the, at times, deeply uncomfortable but honest discussions that this kind of relationship requires, and he was very special. I think it truly does take a lot more than most people realize to defy societal norms when it comes to things like marriage and family.

This was, in part, why it was tremendously hard for me to watch Nette and Zeit—once so vibrant, both as individuals and as a couple—as they were reduced to shells of their former selves. While Zeit still was technically of sound mind, he was confined to a wheelchair and utterly reliant upon a full-time nurse for everything. Because of the conservation, he had to ask permission to do everything, from going to the bathroom to buying a newspaper. Fully aware of what was happening to him, and to Nette, a once proud man was now limp, made impotent by Paula's unwillingness to help find even glimmers of dignity in the conservation.

Eventually, after about nine months, Zeit was moved to a care facility, which only deepened what I assumed was his depression. While his mind remained quite clear, his body steadily continued to decline, and having a more intense level of around-the-clock care made good sense. He wanted desperately to visit Nette, but for reasons I could never quite understand, that request was never honored by the conservator. In a feeble attempt to offer Zeit some comfort, I told him Nette had reached a place in her disease at which she would no longer recognize him but I told her he missed her and was thinking of her. It was mostly, sometimes true. And that was enough. I did not want to further break hearts that were already so broken.

Finally, after nearly a year of intermittent court appearances, the judge was ready to rule on granting custody of Nette to my mother and on moving her to a facility in Chicago. Nette and Zeit had been living apart for nearly a year and a half at that point, but they were each required to be present in court.

The morning of the court appearance, I went to Nette's care facility and dressed her in the most beautiful outfit she had left: a decorated sweatshirt and ill-fitting pants. Given how gorgeous her clothing had once been, to realize this was her "most beautiful" option was bad enough. That she was lucid when I arrived only made it worse. She did not want me to dress her. She did not want to go for a ride in the car.

"Why are you making me get dressed?" she asked as I tried to pull one of the ugly sweatshirts, now her uniform, over her head. "I don't want to go anywhere today—do not touch me!"

Much like a child who did not want to go to school, Nette did not want to cooperate in any way that day.

"I'm taking you for a ride in the car today, Aunt Nette," I said, "so that we can go to see your Neep. Wouldn't you like that?"

Her face softened at the mention of my mother. "My Neep," she said. "I love my Neep, don't I?" Nette called my mother Neep because she said that my mother, as a young child, would always try to "nip" the buttons off her coats and sweaters. Nip became Neep, and it remained so until even that memory eventually faded from Nette's mind.

"Yes. Yes, you do." I took that moment to adjust the sweatshirt and get her arms fully through the sleeves. "And we have to get permission for you to visit your Neep. We are also going to visit with Zeit today. Won't that be nice?"

"I don't know who this Zeit is," she said, "but I would like to see my beloved Alex." Unfortunately, even in her lucid moments, she no longer seemed to know who Zeit was. The only man she remembered was Alex, who she believed had been her husband. That she confused her late brother with her husband was more than sad. It was actually a bit stomach-churning, given how afraid of him I understood her to have been. "Can we visit him today?"

I didn't reply. I never knew quite what to say when this happened, so I focused on getting her dressed and hoped the moment would pass.

With a bit of cajoling from one of the nurses, we managed to get her ready and into the car. Once we were in the car, she suddenly no longer understood what was happening. It was almost as if she lost her balance the moment we left her room, her most familiar place.

She was quiet and stared out the window as we began the drive. But then, after some imperceptible balance had been found, she spoke.

"Is Alex going to be here?" she asked from the back seat. "I want to see Alex."

"Yes. Alex is going to be here. And he's very excited to see you," I relented. And that seemed to keep her calm until we arrived.

Once inside the courtroom, I found out Nette and Zeit were not allowed to sit near each other. "It's not appropriate or necessary," Paula sniped by way of explanation.

I thought it unnecessarily cruel to keep them apart.

"But why?" I asked. "This will be the last time they are ever together if we get approval to move Nette to Chicago. Shouldn't they be allowed to be next to each other a final time?"

"What difference does it make?" said Paula. "Nette doesn't know him anyway."

"But Zeit knows her," I insisted. "And she might know him for a moment. It matters."

I hoped that if there was an ounce of compassion in this horrible woman, it would engage. It did not.

I then asked if we might request to be highest on the docket, given Nette's very fragile condition. She refused. We had to wait our turn—no matter how long that might take or how uncomfortable Nette might be.

I went over to where Zeit sat and tried to explain to him that Paula would not allow them to sit together.

"I just miss her so much . . ."

Zeit's frail voice faltered, and he began to weep. His shoulders slumped. All of his former elegance, grace, and incredible pride gone. I could hardly keep myself from weeping with him.

We waited for nearly an hour, during which I shuttled back and forth between Nette and Zeit. I couldn't sit still, partially out of concern that the judge might refuse our request and partially because it was never comfortable to be around Paula. Or to have Nette out of her facility. Or to see Zeit so horribly sad.

When we were finally called before the judge, Nette sat, tiny in her wheelchair and completely unable to answer any question that might be put to her. I don't remember much of what was said. But in the end, permission was given to move Nette to a facility in Chicago and to give custody of her person—though not her money—to my mother. While the control of Nette's and Zeit's finances remained with Paula, we were allowed to leave.

Paula tried to shuttle Zeit and his caregiver away immediately, but I stopped her. Physically. I stood in her way. "You *will* let them say goodbye," I said. "Zeit needs it. Even if Nette might not. Zeit deserves that much."

Really, he deserved so much more. I pushed their chairs close together, and suddenly Nette knew exactly who she was. And she knew exactly who he was.

"Zeit. My Zeit." She cooed at him as I had seen her do so

many times before. She knew him. Zeit took her hand and kissed it.

"My Nette. You're here."

It felt almost inappropriate to witness a moment so intimate. And so I took a few discreet steps back to try to give them a bit of privacy. I was tremendously grateful that they could share this moment. After forty years together and some of the grandest and most authentic adventures a couple might have, this was the end. And no matter what else may have happened during their marriage, in that moment, there was only love.

Zeit's caregiver came to take him away, and Nette's came for her.

I went to kiss Zeit for what I assumed would be the final time, as he was slipping away far faster now that everything had been stripped from him.

"Thank you, Uncle Zeit," I said. "Thank you for always being so kind to me and my family. For always being so generous. And for taking good care of Nette. You are a wonderful man."

"Thank *you*," he said.

"Do you need anything before we go?"

"I want some money of my own," he said. "A man is not a man without money of his own, Marra."

My bubbie, when I was a young girl, told me the very same thing each time she pinned a five-dollar bill to Uncle

Harold's waistband. So I gave Zeit a hundred-dollar bill I had in my wallet.

Zeit smiled.

"I love you, Uncle Zeit." I leaned down and kissed his cheek again. I knew how much it meant to him to feel that something was only his. And for a man like Zeit, nothing less would have been appropriate. I turned away, tears streaming down my face as I walked to the car.

Someone grabbed my arm. I turned around and saw Paula.

"What did you *do*?" she hissed. "Why on earth would you give him one hundred dollars? That is excessive and unnecessary. I mean, I suppose you can petition the estate to be repaid . . ."

I tuned out as Paula raged on and on at me, utterly clueless as to why even a few moments of dignity matter to the oldest old. Some surrogate daughter she was. That Paula could reduce this moment to a financial discussion left me on the verge of vomiting. But, as I had learned to do by this point, I did not say any of the things I wanted to say.

"There is no need for me to be repaid, Paula," I said. "Have a good afternoon."

Never had getting into the car with Nette been such a refuge.

Nette wept all the way back to her facility. She was withdrawn, her face turned toward the window and her breath peppered with what sounded to me like frustrated sighs.

And yet, at the same time, she did not seem to know exactly what was going on.

"Now I can take you to see your Neep!" I said, glancing at her in the back seat in the rearview mirror. "Won't that be nice?"

"I want to see Alex," she wailed. "Where is my Alex? I want to dance with Alex!"

"You'll see Alex very soon."

What else did it make sense to say at this point?

Chapter Sixteen

THERE ARE MANY THINGS WE IMAGINE DOING IN the name of kindness. Or compassion. For those we love. Even for perfect strangers who are in distress. But when dealing with a family member with advancing Alzheimer's who may or may not think you are the lowest form of human because of your skin color, the world of what you imagine doing grows. Exponentially.

And so it was when it came time to move Nette from San Francisco to Chicago. They may say it's not about the destination; it's about the journey. And the flight to move Nette from San Francisco to Chicago was absolutely that.

Once we were clear to move her, I began to breathe a bit easier at the thought of not having to run back and forth to San Francisco each month and even more at the thought of not having to deal with Nette any longer. I had already decided after the final court date that once the move was complete, I would disengage. While I did not regret anything I had done to that point, I did not feel the need to continue to engage once my mother and sister would be able to manage her care. My mission was soon to be completed, and I could not wait to be free from it all.

Fortunately, there was a rather upscale care facility about five minutes from where both my mother and sister lived. And it had an open bed. All I had to do now was arrange the travel and accompany Nette on the flight.

But Paula wasn't going down without a fight. As she retained control of Nette's finances, any expenditure made on Nette's behalf—from an aspirin to a plane ticket—had to be approved by her.

I recommended that first-class tickets be purchased on the airline with which I had the highest standing. Nette's lifestyle and ability to afford it notwithstanding, being in first class would offer the most limited interaction with other passengers, and should there be any problems, my status with the airline would give us the highest chances of resolving things easily. Nette danced in and out of lucidity, and when she was not lucid, she was often disoriented and violent because of the terror of it all. I did not want to leave anything to chance on the five-hour flight.

Paula did not agree.

"I just don't understand why you're reluctant to stack the

deck in our collective favor," I said. "Isn't it smart all around to try to ensure the most comfortable flight for Nette?"

I was playing a verbal game of chess with Paula, trying to checkmate or perhaps shame her into seeing things my way.

"First class just seems excessive," she replied. "I know that *you* believe in it, but I don't."

In her own inimitable way, Paula believed this was my attempt to make sure I was comfortable and travelling in the fanciest possible way. She never resisted an opportunity to accuse me of wrongdoing and selfishness, which I always found to be divinely ironic, given that she was the one controlling everything, and I had spent—quite literally—thousands of my own dollars to finance every trip to California for the last two years.

"I do believe in it," I told her. "But so did Nette and Zeit. In fact, I learned it from them. And if Nette were able to choose, this is how she would want it too."

Checkmate.

The first-class tickets were purchased, and an end date for this adventure was at last in sight. The plan was that Paula would pick us up at Nette's facility and drive us to the airport so that she could have a final goodbye. Given how infrequently she actually spent time with Nette—less often than I did each month—I found it dramatic and a bit nauseating, but I did not argue. I could not wait to leave San Francisco in my rearview mirror and get Nette to Chicago.

Nette's doctor suggested giving her a sedative so that she might be as comfortable as possible on the flight. While I had never taken a sedative of any kind, I was secretly hoping he would also give me one, for any change of environment at that point was a source of deep distress for Nette—and therefore a nightmare for me.

When we arrived at the airport, Paula made quite a show when saying goodbye to Nette. With tears in her eyes, she bent down to give Nette a feeble hug.

"I love you, Nette," she said. "Be well." I could barely contain my laughter. She then turned her beady eyes to me and said, "And you'd better take good care of this special lady."

It was all I could do not to roll my eyes. Even with the move to Chicago, I would be tied to Paula through her control of Nette's finances until Nette's death, and I did not want to do anything to further inflame an already challenging relationship.

"We cannot thank you enough for your care and attention to both Nette and Zeit, Paula," I said. And with a limp handshake, she went her way and we went ours. Thankfully, this was the last time I would have to see her in person.

Just before going through security, I took out Nette's sedative, as the doctor had instructed. The hope was that it would reach full potency by the time we were settled into our seats.

"We are going on an airplane to see Alex," I told her.

"Won't that be fun?" It was like talking to a small child at this point, and Alex was the only name she seemed able to hold on to.

"I love Alex," she whispered.

"And he loves you," I said. "Very much. He cannot wait to see you. Now be a good girl; take your medicine, and we will go to the plane."

She was very calm that day, and she took the sedative without complaint. I was convinced things were going to go beautifully.

But then we got to the security check, and a TSA officer tried to insist I get Nette out of her wheelchair to walk through the metal detector unassisted and then remove her shoes for further screening. To say this was impossible is an understatement. She would not allow strangers to touch her, let alone strangers who showed no gentleness or empathy toward her. Nette grew agitated while I did my best to both protect her and get a supervisor to hear me out. The entire scene was chaotic at best.

"Do you *honestly* think this frail, ninety-year-old, wheelchair-bound woman with Alzheimer's is a terrorist!?" Words I never thought I would have to say to another human being came flying out of my mouth. Nonsensical at best. But that's where we were. "Here is a letter from her doctor," I insisted. I decided to switch back to the game of verbal chess I had played with Paula, hoping that some sense of empathy would kick in. *"Look at her.* Please. Let's leave her in the chair and not agitate her. She's sick enough as it is."

Eventually, they relented, and we made it to the gate and onto the plane.

Tucked into the first row of the plane, with Nette in the window seat, I informed the flight attendants of the situation. "My aunt has advanced Alzheimer's, so don't feel the need to ask her if she wants or needs anything," I told them. "I've given her a strong sedative, and I'm sure she'll sleep for much of the flight. And if she doesn't, I'll take care of her. Thank you in advance for your understanding."

"You're such a sweet girl to take care of her like this," the flight attendant said.

"You have no idea," I thought to myself.

"Thank you so much," I said aloud.

Then I settled in for the flight.

Did you know that, on rare occasions, certain medications have the opposite of the intended effect on the person taking them? I know for a couple of reasons. First, because I am one of the lucky creatures who often reacts badly to medication, and the only way to find out is to have the adverse reaction play out. For me, that happened when I was given Vicodin after gallbladder surgery, and I vomited violently until it had been purged from my body.

Second, I know because when the sedative I gave Nette did reach full potency, as the plane was taking off, it became clear that it was not having the effect of a sedative. Instead, Nette became agitated. Horribly, loudly agitated. To make matters worse, she did not recognize me and did not under-stand why a perfect stranger was talking to her, touching her, and trying to calm her down.

"Who are you?" Nette screamed, her eyes wild and her voice shrill. I tried to pat her arm to calm her. "Do not *touch* me!" she wailed. "DO NOT LET THIS STRANGER TOUCH ME!"

I had never felt as trapped or helpless as I did on that plane. But all I could do was my best under extraordinary and unfortunate circumstances. When we boarded, I knew that the flight attendants and my fellow passengers assumed I was a professional caregiver, employed to take care of Nette in this way. Little did they know that I was far from it. As she was belted in, I was free to move about the cabin. I im-mediately made my way to each row, explaining the situation to my fellow cabinmates. "My aunt has Alzheimer's, and her medication is not working properly," I told them. "I apol-ogize, as we are sure to interrupt the quiet on this flight. I appreciate your understanding." Row after row, I did my best to lay the groundwork for as much peace and patience as pos-sible. For all of us.

Although it was only 10:30 a.m., one of the flight atten-dants offered me a scotch when I got back to my seat.

"Here, honey," she said, "I think you're going to need this."

"Thanks so much, but no. I'll be fine," I told her. "We will be just fine, won't we, Aunt Nette?"

"Do not let this stranger talk to me!" Nette pleaded to the flight attendant. OK. *Not* fine.

The flight attendant looked at me, both compassionately and slightly incredulously, as if to say, "Are you sure you don't want a drink?" But I declined again, thinking it would be best to have all of my wits about me.

About halfway through the flight, Nette had to go to the bathroom.

"I have to make pee-pee and poo-poo," she told me. "Pretty lady, I have to make." I never quite grew accustomed to hearing Nette speak in a language different from the clipped, condescending tone she had always used with me. At least I was "pretty lady" this time.

"May I help you?" I asked her. "I think you might need some help, and I would really love to help you. My name is Marra."

By some small miracle, I managed to get her to agree to let me help her into the tiny airplane lavatory and settle her onto the toilet, but before she could actually sit down—yes, with the lavatory door slightly ajar since we both could not fit into the small space and close the door—she lost control of her bowels. And it went absolutely everywhere.

Somehow, she managed to avoid getting it on her pants, but the need to clean both her and the bathroom cannot be understated. I took a look around. There was no space and there were no resources to do a proper job of cleaning. She began to cry. And so did I.

"I'm *sorry*," she cried. Tears ran down her cheeks. It was heartbreaking.

"It's OK," I said, trying in vain to wipe away my own tears. "It's not your fault. I'll clean you up and everything will be OK." And I went about the business of cleaning her up as one does a child who accidentally soils herself, all the while whispering that it was all going to be OK and that it wasn't her fault. Because it wasn't. My only resource was the cheap, single-ply toilet paper that disintegrates when water hits it, but I did the best I could.

I could feel all the eyes in the first-class cabin upon me, from passengers to flight attendants, as I put Nette back in her seat. I then went about the task, on my hands and knees, of trying to clean up the mess left in the lavatory. And I did it without gloves. Usually, I don't even wash dishes without gloves, but there I was. Gloveless. And cleaning the airplane bathroom.

It would not have been fair to expect the flight attendants to do it, and they did not offer. They gave me what they could—cloth napkins from the lunch trays and the warm towels that are handed out just after takeoff—and stood by, watching.

The job was absolutely mine. I had taken it on when I had decided that the goal was to move Nette to Chicago, and this was now a part of that job. I have done many things in my life as acts of care, but getting on my hands and knees to clean feces off the floor of an airplane lavatory tops the list of things from which I may never recover.

Even more repulsive than the filth was seeing a once elegant, well-travelled woman who had always held herself with the energy of royalty reduced to this. And knowing that it would only get worse from here broke my heart. The indignity of the moment was not lost on me on any front.

Once I had cleaned things as best I could, I sat on the floor of the galley and openly wept.

"I'll take that scotch now," I said. And the laughter finally came. Through the tears. But it came.

Miraculously, Nette fell asleep for the remainder of the flight, and I sat in filthy, exhausted silence, praying for the flight to be over.

My mother and sister met us at baggage claim, and I gratefully handed Nette over to them. I could not bring myself to share the exact details of the flight immediately. Even with all of my regular business travel, nothing could have prepared me for this single horrific, exhausting flight. I just wanted to go home, to the comfort of my mother's kitchen, a very hot shower, and my bed. And I assumed that was the plan. That they would take me home first and then take Nette to get her settled into her new facility.

My sister, unaware of how traumatizing the trip had been, had other ideas.

"So you'll come with us to get Aunt Nette settled into her new home," she said as we made our way to the car. "And then you'll come over to my house for dinner. The kids want to see you, and I want to hear all about the trip. So let's get going."

I looked at her and said, far more loudly than I should have, "You know how they say, 'Shit happens'? Well, it did. Nette shit all over herself on the flight, and I had to clean her. And the airplane bathroom. On my hands and knees. Take. Me. Home. *Now.*"

You could have heard a pin drop, and in retrospect, even I fully appreciate the tragicomic genius of the moment. My mother, with both complete compassion in her voice and laughter in her eyes, quietly put her hand on my shoulder and said, "I'm so sorry, sweetheart. We will take you home. You are done now. And we will find a way to thank you."

"*Thank you*, Mama. I really need to go home. Right now."

When I was finally alone and had taken a very long shower, I crawled into bed, alternating between sobs and deep breaths—utterly convinced that, after eighteen months, I was done.

And for that moment, I was.

Chapter Seventeen

THERE WAS A MOMENT EARLY ON IN THE ADVENTURE with Nette's conservation and disease when I started to wrap my brain around the truly enormous task I had undertaken. I never really understood what was going to come next, and I was truly out of my depth most of the time. I was unsure about almost everything. Except one thing.

I was absolutely, unwaveringly sure that once Nette was moved to the facility near my mother, I was done. I was not going to visit. I was not going to help, and I was not going to feel bad about it. The facility was a five-minute drive from both my mother and my sister, and I made it clear to them at every possible turn that I was done. Nette was their job from here forward.

And I really believed that to be true. I needed time and space to process everything. My friends and colleagues thought I was crazy to become the caregiver for a clearly racist woman who had never held any warmth or love for me—I wanted to make sure I didn't also think I was crazy.

But my mother was still recovering from what turned out to be thirteen kidney procedures, and it was best for all concerned that she not drive or be out and about on her own. So, more often than not, I found myself driving her to the facility. My mother never asked me if I wanted to come in. She knew I did not. Instead, I sat on a bench outside. And I ate ice cream—Nette's care facility faced a Culver's. As I had come to know very early in life and much to my dismay, ice cream can be very comforting when one is contemplating things. Especially when contemplating the eighteen months I had just lived.

The routine was almost always the same.

"Do you need anything, Marra?"

"No, Mama. I'm fine. I'll be sitting out here when you're done with your visit. I hope she's having a good day."

And then I would get my ice cream, usually something involving M&M's, and sit. Thinking. In spite of myself because I really didn't want to think about it. Nor did I want to relive any of it. And yet, I did. Each visit to California. Each painful interaction with Nette when she was lucid. The ongoing battle with horrible Paula. Zeit's decline and my helplessness where he was concerned. The trips to court. The oceans of tears I had cried while en route to the Four Seasons after each visit to Nette's care facility.

On the ride home after my mother's visit, I would politely ask how Nette was doing. We would then go back to our lives. I appreciated so very much that my mother never pressured me about anything when it came to Nette. She made it clear she did not expect me to ever go in to see her. And that I had already done more than enough.

One afternoon, a few months after Nette's return to Chicago, I found myself asking more questions on the short ride from the facility to my mother's home.

"I mean . . . has she changed much?"

"How has she changed? Is she still talking baby talk like she was when I brought her back?"

"Can she walk without assistance?"

"Does she know you anymore?"

Clearly, I wanted to know. And so I decided that next time, I would get off the bench and go in to see things for myself. As the day approached, I found myself terrified. After everything I'd been through, I wanted to see Nette. I couldn't, for the life of me, understand why. My job was done. Nette was well cared for and was being attended to by my mother and sister. There was no reason for me to be in the mix.

But I wanted to know. I wanted to see her. I felt like I needed to properly finish what I had started, and never seeing her again would leave it unfinished for me. I felt a bit guilty that I hadn't gone sooner. And I'm not sure what I expected to find.

I talked it through with my mother, and we ultimately decided it would be best if I went alone. So much had happened in California that was just between Nette and me. As ugly as it was, it was between us—and that is how I felt it should remain.

When I walked into the facility, I was immediately struck by how different it was from the one in which she'd lived in California. California had been dark. Small. Sparse. The only similarity was the locked doors. Alzheimer's facilities or floors are carefully locked so the residents can't leave the building or ward. Once I passed through the locked doors, the world was bright. Like a primary school classroom.

Each door had either a flower or a sports ball on it with the name of the resident who lived therein. The arts and crafts room was similar to the one in my niece's preschool, with crayons, craft paper, markers, and coloring books strewn about. And music from another time was softly playing. The juxtaposition of music from the 1940s and the childlike amenities struck me as being all at once sad and sweet, much like many of the residents.

I found Nette sitting in her bedroom, which was small but brightly decorated. She had a twin bed with a railing on the side. The railing was less like a hospital bed rail and more like the one parents put on the side of a toddler's bed so that their child doesn't fall out in the middle of the night.

There were pictures of our family everywhere, provided by my sister, and Nette was sitting in a chair looking out the window.

"Nette . . . ?" I softly called her name, and she turned to look at me.

There was no recognition there. Not even a glimmer. Toward the end of Nette's time in California, she had drifted in and out of awareness, but at some point during almost every visit, she'd known who I was. Not so any longer.

I walked farther into the room, and she continued to look at me with a sad, vacant stare.

I crouched down next to her and said, "It's Marra. I've come for a visit."

"You're a pretty lady," she said, just as she had in California. "I'd like a visit with you."

It was divinely, and bitterly, ironic that only in her state of dementia did she find me to be beautiful.

"Are you happy here?"

"Of course I am." She smiled. "This is a *very* nice hotel!"

And so it was to her. In the smallest and loveliest way, the part of the old Nette who loved very nice hotels was in this Nette, turning the care facility into something palatable where she belonged.

My mother had warned me that Nette had deteriorated to the point where she almost never recognized anyone anymore, but I was still unprepared for it. I kept waiting for the

Nette I had always known to reappear, as she had in California. But she never did. For the first time that I knew, the disease had completely overtaken her. No matter who she had ever been, this disease was one of the most heartbreaking ways to die that I had ever witnessed—even as it continued to change her into a sweet soul.

I took her for a walk down to the television room, and we sat for a bit. I still could not bear to be there longer than about forty-five minutes, and fortunately, it was then time for her to be taken down for dinner.

"It's time for you to have dinner with your friends," I told Nette. "I'll see you again soon." I gave her a kiss on her cheek, which she happily accepted—for the first time in either of our lives.

I think two things can happen when one finds one's most peaceful center, especially if food and body image issues were ever a part of one's nonpeaceful life.

You can get bigger. And you can get smaller.

For me, finding my peace has meant getting smaller. Literally.

For decades, I have joked that my weight, much like the late, very great Luther Vandross's before me, has gone through wild fluctuations. Meant with no offense to the incredible Mr. Vandross, whose music has been a part of the soundtrack of my life forever. After ballooning to a number on the scale that arbitrarily pushed me over the edge, I would seek a new solution. There is not a diet I have not tried. Weight Watchers. Jenny Craig. Nutrisystem.

I tried, in vain, to make myself vomit after meals, as I had seen other girls do at school. Thankfully, I wasn't at all comfortable with that. But I would try absolutely anything to get the weight off. And then, when I reached a comfortable lower weight, something would inevitably happen to send me back to my beloved chocolate cake in the middle of the night. For one reason or another, I wanted to once again retreat into the safety of invisibility.

This was my cycle for years.

And it was not until last year, when I really delved into the reasons for my desired invisibility, that I allowed the weight to come off me in a way that was gentle. Loving. I no longer eat as a way to punish myself. Or my body.

And so, my sense of peace has made my body smaller. And my heart bigger.

For Nette, it was the opposite.

After nine decades of obsessively watching her weight, denying herself any pleasure when it came to food, and berating others for their bodies and their food choices, Nette had started to eat. With relish. To this day, I marvel at the freedoms that Alzheimer's brought to Nette's day-to-day life. And the freedom to eat without guilt was certainly one of them.

For so many, the disease creates an unlikable stranger out

of a loved one, someone you do not want to know. For me, it was the opposite, but it took me a while to accept what had happened. Even with my mother and Nette's caregivers telling me for weeks that Nette was no longer the woman we knew and that she was rarely lucid at this point, I didn't believe them. Every time I looked at her, abusive moments would come flooding back to me, taking my system back in time, even though the woman I was sitting with had, for all intents and purposes, been transformed into a new person. I could not escape the past.

My mother told me that if I just shared a meal with Nette, I would understand how different she really was.

After much back-and-forth, I decided to make another visit to do just that.

I went up to Nette's floor, where I found her in the TV room with her friends. I always loved that the TV room did not show current television shows. Rather, the facility showed tapes of very early television, programs the residents often were able to remember. That's the thing about Alzheimer's. It's so complex. And one never knows when a memory will resonate.

We watched two episodes of *The Mary Tyler Moore Show*—which had always been a favorite of mine—and chatted with her friends for a bit. Like Nette, the ladies were all in advanced stages of the disease, and so they had all settled into an almost childlike place. Visiting with them was similar to watching my seven-year-old niece play with her friends. They giggled and clapped their hands when they found something funny. It was adorable, although to be honest, I found it a bit unsettling when compared to the Nette I had always known.

At some point, Nette turned to me and said, "I want a snack!"

The comment caught me off guard. It's not that she hadn't eaten when she was healthy. She had. But it was almost the same thing each day, measured out with extreme precision, and each bite was explicitly designed to both give her enough energy to get her through the day—and not make her gain even an ounce. Eighty-nine pounds was always the magic number.

But this Nette wanted a snack.

The care facility's dining room was much like a restaurant for the residents, and when family members visited, residents would often take their loved ones there to sit and chat in whatever way was possible. So we took a trip down to find a snack.

"Chocolate cake!" she exclaimed as we got settled at a table.

This Nette wanted chocolate cake.

"Then I will get you some." I smiled. The dining room had a fabulous buffet, and there was more than enough cake to go around.

When I put the plate down in front of her, she smiled and clapped, exclaiming, "I *love* chocolate cake!"

To say that she ate with relish would be an understatement. She dug in. Nette ate that piece of cake with more joy than I had ever seen her show doing anything. She had frosting on her face. Cake crumbs everywhere. It was the absolute opposite of the way she used to eat: in tiny bites, never dropping so much as a crumb anywhere and never getting food all over herself.

But then came a question.

"Would you like some of my cake? It's yummy!" she said. "And since we are friends, I can share it with you."

I almost cried.

She considered us to be friends? She was willing to share? She was encouraging me to eat fattening cake? No abusive comments about girls like me being smart not to eat cake?

She was indeed transformed.

"I would love some cake."

I got a fork, and we shared what was left of her piece. I don't think I had ever in my life enjoyed a few bites of cake that much.

At the time of her death, Nette had gained almost ten pounds, which was substantial on her tiny frame. Her cheeks were full. Her belly was a bit round. And I found myself hoping she enjoyed every bite that those ten pounds represented as much as she had enjoyed the cake on that afternoon.

Chapter Eighteen

My visits with Nette became more frequent. I found myself wanting to spend more time with her. I wanted to see how she was changing. I wanted to see how she was, if at all, remaining the same. I wanted to see how *we* were changing.

I went alone to visit.

"Her room is small," I would tell myself. There wasn't room for my mother, my sister, and me to visit at the same time. "If we all go on different days, she will have visitors almost every day," became another rationalizing refrain. And wasn't it better for her to have visitors daily rather than a few times per week?

But the truth was that I wanted to be alone with her. No matter what might happen on any given day, so much good and bad had transpired just between the two of us, and I wanted these moments to be the same.

One afternoon, I decided I would go specifically because it was Ballroom Dance Day at the facility. I had found myself doing more and more research about Alzheimer's—about what sorts of things might be beneficial to those living with the disease. Almost everything I read suggested it was worthwhile to try to engage the patient in activities that used to resonate deeply. If anyone would want to be the dancing queen, it would be Nette.

Nette studied dance during her younger years, and when she met Zeit, her dancing went to the next level when they took on ballroom dance as a couple. They competed in the senior citizen divisions of dance competitions in San Francisco. It was yet another thing that made her seem so glamorous and beautiful, and there was nothing she enjoyed more than putting on a dance show.

When my brother was around ten years old and presumably able to follow, I remember that she tried to teach him how to dance the fox-trot during one of her annual visits. Nette and Zeit had turned the basement of their home into a dance studio, where Nette often gave lessons. She believed that the ability to dance "properly" was important and that it was especially important for a man to know how to lead. I cannot help but wonder if she thought that a metaphor for the failure of many of her marriages.

As she was so petite and my brother was taller than average, their heights were almost perfectly matched, even at his young age. In a strange accent that she only used when she was dancing, she instructed him. "This is the *fox-trot*," she said. "And the pattern we will do is qvick, qvick, slow . . . qvick, qvick, slow . . ."

Awkwardly, my brother did his best to oblige. It was sweet, and as ever, I found myself wishing that somehow I might be able to dance with Nette.

"May I have a turn, Aunt Nette?" I was always asking some version of that question.

"I can't teach you the woman's part," she snapped. "A man has to teach you." And with that, she turned her body and her attention back to my brother and their dance lesson.

Little did Nette know, I had recently started taking ballroom dance lessons—and had taken my own turn as the queen of the dance floor. *Dancing with the Stars* had become a television sensation, and ballroom dance had become quite chic for young people to learn. And, very quickly, I learned two things. First, Nette was right. It is better that a man teach a woman how to partner and a woman teach a man. In spite of myself, I had to admit that this was true. The second thing I learned was that the pattern for the fox-trot is not "qvick, qvick, slow." It is slow, slow, quick, quick. I had gone into my fox-trot lesson armed with Nette's voice in my head and sure that I would impress my charming teacher, only to find that Nette had taught my brother, and in turn me, incorrectly.

"Honey," my gorgeous instructor had said, "who taught you that? She didn't know what she was talking about!"

I laughed heartily. He had no idea how true that was.

That afternoon on Ballroom Dance Day, I thought it might be my time to twirl with Nette. And secretly, I hoped they would play the ABBA classic "Dancing Queen," which had been one of my favorite songs since childhood. At some point in 1976, my family went on a driving vacation. While I don't recall our destination, I do recall that our entire family stayed in one hotel room. That meant that my bubbie and I shared a cot. Yes, a cot that was brought in as an extra bed. I loved to curl up with my bubbie under any circumstance, and a small hotel cot was certainly no exception. One night during this particular road trip, we ended up watching a TV movie very late at night while the rest of the family slept. And snored.

The film was called *Queen of the Stardust Ballroom*, and it starred Maureen Stapleton and Charlotte Rae, who had been a classmate of my bubbie's. The film was about a woman who had lost her husband and found solace in ballroom dance at a local dance hall. I don't remember much, but I do remember that at the end of the film, she was named the Queen of the Stardust Ballroom and "Dancing Queen" played. When I hear it, I both miss my bubbie terribly and want to twirl under a disco ball.

I found Nette, as I normally did, in her room. Even with her belly getting rounder, Nette seemed smaller to me each time I visited. It was like her body was vanishing along with her memory, which would eventually leave nothing but a shell of each.

"It's dance day, Aunt Nette," I said. "Would you like to dance today?"

"I don't know how to dance, pretty lady. I don't know how."

But I knew better.

I wheeled Nette down to the multipurpose room, which would be our dance studio for the afternoon. While she seemed to enjoy watching the other residents dance, she did not want to actually get up and try to dance herself. She sat in her chair and applauded.

"Look at them twirl!" she exclaimed, as ever, with the wonder and appreciation of a child.

"Won't you come and try it with us? We will go slow." The instructors tried to get her up and onto the dance floor, but she shook her head and declined decidedly.

"I do not know *how* to dance," she insisted. It broke my heart. I took her back to her room and told her I would come back another day.

About two weeks later, I decided I would try to remind Nette that she not only knew how to dance but was also the dancing queen. I brought a boom box and a Rosemary Clooney CD with me to her facility. I wanted to see if she might engage with the music one-on-one. I turned it on at a soft volume, and I said, "Aunt Nette, you do know how to dance. You love dancing. And you are so good at it that you used to teach other people how to dance."

She didn't say anything. She just sat and stared at me intently, listening to every word I said in a way that I'm not sure she ever had before.

"You weren't just a dancer," I said. "You were a champion. You were the queen of the stardust ballroom." Calling her the queen made her smile. "Won't you please try to have a dance with me?"

"I'll try," she said.

And so, we did.

I put on "You Make Me Feel So Young." Rosemary Clooney's version is a perfect fox-trot. I gently helped Nette up out of her chair, lifting her shrinking body up to its full height. I took on the male position and drew her into my arms. Once upon a time, the thought of touching me, of being close to me, of being in my dancer's embrace would have been utterly unthinkable to her. Probably even repugnant. But this Nette thought me beautiful and sweet, and I had become appealing and comforting to her.

"We are going to try the fox-trot," I said. "The pattern is slow, slow . . . quick, quick."

After a few clumsy minutes, Nette snapped into sharp lucidity. She feebly pushed me away and said, "*No*. It is qvick, qvick . . . slow. Do it right if you're going to do it."

There she was. The old Nette. Fierce. Mean. And always, always, always sure she was right. I knew she was in there somewhere.

Clearly, the research was correct. There was something in the dancing that did bring Nette back. And even though she was cross for a moment, she was again the dancer (and the instructor) she had been once upon a time.

The lucidity didn't last long, and we did not dance while it did. But once she faded back into her happier fog, I took her back into my arms, and we took a twirl.

And for that afternoon, if only for a few brief moments, we were both the queens of the ballroom.

Chapter Nineteen

"WHAT SHOULD WE TALK ABOUT TODAY?"

Nette was silent. She had been slowly creeping toward total silence for a few weeks at that point, but that day, the quiet was full. And her eyes were blank. There was no smiling. There was nothing.

I knew from my seemingly constant research that eventually, Alzheimer's patients stop speaking because they cannot remember how. And then, their bodies stop breathing, presumably for the same reason.

It was happening. And from my vantage point, it was time to let Nette go.

So often, people cling to their loved ones toward the end of their lives. Perhaps because they are not ready to say goodbye. Perhaps because they fear what death looks like. Perhaps because they cannot imagine what happens in the life that goes on without their loved one in it. And so, they cling.

The opposite seems to happen with pets, who are put to sleep because it is more humane to send them off gently than to have them suffer. I've never understood why the same does not apply to humans. And I know I am not alone in that confusion.

Of course, to watch someone you love suffer with illness is a different kind of pain—and it creates an unwinnable war within. Do you choose to let them go, knowing it will mean the end of their suffering? Or do you beg them to hold on, praying for a miracle that might never come?

I am a girl who doesn't just believe in miracles; I exist because of them. But I know all too well that there are times when death is the most humane option.

Often, it is our sick loved ones who are holding on—for us. Often, they don't want to leave us because they know there will be pain and sadness that they will no longer be able to help soften. And that pain will be about them.

Sometimes, we have to give our loved ones permission to die.

Having seen death quite close before I was twenty-three years old, I came to believe early on that there is real compassion in this permission; it's an acknowledgment—made together—that a new phase of life is about to begin through death.

When it was my father's time, I did not have the words or the strength to actually say it. But I did pray, from the deepest place in my heart, for God to take him. My father had been reduced to a shadow—quiet and unable to do anything other than lie in a bed, stoned out of his mind on the opium they gave him to help manage the pain. He was not living. And he did not want to exist in a state like that.

I could not say the words to him—but I did say them to God.

When it was my bubbie's time, I had the words. And I kept the promise I had first made to her as a child and told her it was time. We even had a laugh about it.

I decided it was time to tell Nette the same thing. She was languishing, trapped inside a body and a mind that were barely holding on. She had outstayed her time at the party, as my bubbie would say.

When I was a young girl, Bubbie would pepper our conversations with lessons about what it meant to be a lady. A lady always keeps her knees together, for example. While I'm sure she meant this metaphorically, she also meant it quite literally. To "sit like a lady" was very important to her, and Bubbie did not shrink from pointing out how inelegant it was when one did not comply. At my Hebrew school graduation, a girl in a dress sat on the *bimah*, which is a synagogue's equivalent of an altar, with her legs spread wide, and to this day, even with Bubbie gone for more than twenty years, my family thinks of that poor girl and Bubbie's thinly veiled outrage over her choice of position in front of God and everyone.

A lady always wears a slip under her dress or skirt. And that slip must be a color that closely matches the outer garment. I broke this cardinal rule at my bat mitzvah, where I chose to wear a black slip under my pale lavender skirt. Trust me when I say that I never lived that down, and for years thereafter, Bubbie did not hesitate to check under my clothing to make sure I had chosen the right slip.

A lady also, my bubbie believed, always knows when it's time to leave the party.

To her, to stay too long at a party meant you did not have a sense of where you belonged and did not care about your reputation. To her generation, the late hours at a party were when the darker deeds took place, and that was no place for a lady. It should be said that Bubbie was right.

For Nette, the party had been coming to an excruciating end for quite some time. She barely moved, and when she did, it was with deliberate assistance. And now, she was silent. She had not spoken in weeks. Much like babies follow the voices of people who speak to them and smile, so too did she. We weren't quite sure she understood anything we said, but I had the distinct feeling she did and was simply taking it all in. As is the case with Alzheimer's, one never really knows what is going on inside the head of the patient.

After the silent visit with Nette, I debated discussing my thoughts with my mother and sister, but in the end, I decided against it. No one really ever wants to discuss an impending death, and we were no different. We were still living with painfully visceral memories of what happened when we lost my father and Bubbie. Really, we still are. To have to discuss another one seemed cruel and unfair. This was not my first rodeo. My mind was made up. And I knew what I wanted to say. I did not feel like I needed permission to say it.

Armed with a small piece of chocolate cake, I went for a visit, and I spoke the words I had been rehearsing in my mind. Even knowing what I wanted and needed to say, it was harder than I had anticipated to tell this silent, childlike woman that I thought it was time for her to leave the party.

We went down to the dining room, and I tucked us into a corner table and put the chocolate cake down in front of Nette. Mary Poppins had it right—I was convinced that a spoonful of sugar might help the afternoon go better for both of us.

"I've brought you a treat, Aunt Nette. Your favorite. Chocolate cake."

She stared blankly at me and managed a weak, almost imperceptible smile. She allowed me to feed her tiny bites of cake, but she was barely able to chew. As she ate, I gently rubbed her back, feeling the bones poking through her thin skin, and I began to softly whisper near her ear.

"We have all been so happy to have you here with us," I said. "To have had so much time with you. But you and my bubbie taught me that a lady always knows when it is time to leave the party. I want you to know that we will be OK if you decide it's time for you to take your leave."

Without warning, Nette snapped into lucidity, something we had not seen for many weeks. "Young lady," she quipped as sharply as her weak, shaky voice allowed, "I will decide when it is time for me to leave the party." Her eyes narrowed. "That is not for you to say."

There she was. The old Nette. Defiant. Deliberate. She was in there.

And then, just as quickly as the old Nette had shown up, she disappeared again. Nette became silent. And waited for me to feed her the next crumbs of cake.

I'm not sure if she knew I was the person suggesting she leave the party. I'm not sure she knew at all where she was— or even what had transpired moments beforehand.

But she heard me. And she did not like what I had to say.

Those were the last words Nette spoke. At least to me. And in that respect, she absolutely had the last word. Just as she would have wanted it.

When a family member, even a very challenging one, is gravely ill and in their final days, there is a seemingly endless wait for the phone call that confirms the journey toward death has been completed. For some reason, I had always believed that those calls came at night. The call that my father was gone came under the cover of night. When my bubbie left us, I was in the room, but even so, she left us in darkness.

But when Nette died, after years of her march into the deepest parts of Alzheimer's, the call came in at around five a.m.—the morning after I had my chat with her about knowing when to leave the party.

Perhaps she had heard me after all.

I was en route to New York that morning, so I was already awake when the call came.

"Yes," I heard my mother say in her barely awake voice. "I understand. When did it happen? I understand. I'm on my way."

"She's gone, isn't she?" Unless someone is having a baby, five a.m. calls really only mean one thing.

"She is," my mother said. "They said she went in her sleep. They found her when they did their early morning bed check."

"We should go," I said, and before there was even a drop of coffee, we went to the care facility so that we might begin to handle the business that accompanies death.

We found Nette lying lifeless in her twin bed in her room. She was petite while she lived, but in her death, she was tiny. We found her in the fetal position. Uncovered. Cold. Her skin blue.

I have seen death inhabit many bodies. And there is some truth to the notion that someone whose soul has left their body simply looks asleep. So it was with my father, who retained his warmth even after his soul had left his body; he looked so peaceful. Not so with Nette. She looked like what those who have never seen death fear it will look like. Ghostly pale. Tight. Cold. Frozen. As if one touch might turn her to dust. The sight of her left me as cold as she often had when she was alive.

If Nette could have seen herself, she would have been devastated to look so horrible. I almost wanted to fix her hair and put some lipstick on her. But I could barely stand to look at her body. The thought of touching her was more than I could stand.

I would be lying if I said I didn't breathe a sigh of relief when the realization set in that she was finally gone. The suffering, for both of us, was now at an end. And she did suffer, I think, before and after Alzheimer's took residence inside her. But I would also be lying if I didn't acknowledge a part of me that was sad that, in the end, she was left like this. After everything that had been said and done, we had found a place where we finally connected, and even if it was driven by her dementia, I had finally found a place of peace, comfort, and, at times, even joy in her company. And that, too, was now gone.

"You should go to New York, Marra," my mother urged

me. "Your sister is here. We will handle this." She knew I had a big meeting at Deutsche Bank for which I had been preparing for a few weeks. And, ever practical, she did not want me to miss it.

"If you're sure, Mama . . ." My voice trailed off. I did not argue with her. I wanted to go. Still, I stood in the room a few moments longer, debating whether or not I wanted to kiss Nette's cheek as I had kissed my father and Bubbie when they died. In the end, I decided against it.

"I love you," I said. "And I'll call you when I get to the city. If you need me to come back, I'll be on the next plane. I love you." I hugged my mother and my sister as fully as my arms and heart would stretch. And I left.

I am not embarrassed to say I was relieved to be leaving and grateful to have some time in a city that has always left me feeling fully alive. I took my place in the conference room on Wall Street and did my best to focus on the deal that was on the table. It was a deal I had orchestrated, and I was really proud to have this moment in an arena I had never dreamed I would enter. But I was not wholly there. Not in the conference room. Not at the gorgeous dinner my investors hosted to celebrate the deal. And so I wrapped up my business quickly and returned to Chicago.

As personal as things were when Nette was alive—painful, enlightening, and maddening—the immediate business of death can be decidedly impersonal.

There were papers to sign, arrangements to be made, and deep breaths to be taken. I knew what this looked like; when we lost my father, I was intricately involved in managing the process, even at only nineteen years old. That said, I felt only slightly guilty that I was not helping now.

When I arrived in New York, it had struck me that even with the uncomfortable combination of being both busy and distracted, I was sitting still and breathing deeply in a way I had not since my grand adventure began. Even the enjoyable moments with Nette in the final months of her life had been stressful to me. I just didn't realize it fully until she was gone. I was probably always waiting for her bite to return, and I held that in my body. In my breath. But now, no matter what else I had thought or felt, I was at peace. And I inhaled and exhaled with clear awareness of that peace.

Being no stranger to death and her aftermath, I had a set of expectations going into Nette's. But much like anything that was unique to Nette, my expectations were quickly blown out of the water. The order of funeral proceedings, which I knew so well since the order is the same for every Jewish person, did not apply to Nette. She had made her own very specific arrangements years prior, and there would not be a funeral of any kind for a few months. As had become the norm with Nette, my family had to find their way through an unusual process after managing her care under equally unusual circumstances.

Nette's belongings had been cleaned out when she was conserved. And by cleaned out, I mean pilfered from before being sent to my mother. Her best jewelry was gone. Her furs were gone too. While we will never know who did the pilfering, what we do know is that no one was "minding the store."

With considerable work on my end to find a real estate agent and to get the work done to make it presentable, the house had been sold nearly two years ago, just a few months prior to the judge giving us permission to move Nette. And the few things she had had in her room at the care facility— the bed and dresser and her clothing—my mother and sister decided to leave in case someone else might need them. There was nothing left to do on that front.

What was left was the excruciating task of the will and trust. Zeit had died a few months before Nette, and since my mother had been named executor of both Nette's and Zeit's wills, there was now a great deal of work for her to manage. Boxes of Nette's things had been arriving from San Francisco for months, as Paula had taken her time in sending over things she didn't feel were "essential." But now they were all arriving at the same time. Hastily packed. Broken. Unlabeled. Box after box arrived. It seemed to be never-ending, and it was yet another reminder of the sad state of disrepair Nette's life had fallen into during her later years.

The documents around the will and trust numbered nearly one hundred pages, with very specific instructions about every penny. And there was money left, even with Paula's seemingly absent accounting practices. In spite of what I had always experienced as her extreme selfishness, Nette was deeply devoted to several charities, including one that was specific to dachshunds. Nette and Zeit had had two dachshunds that they had loved deeply and treated very much like their children, and their trust clearly wanted that love to be shared after their deaths. There were education charities that were meaningful to Zeit and dance-related ones that were meaningful to them both. Fortunately, the process was quite smooth, all things considered. And then all we had left was simply to schedule, a couple of months later, Nette's burial in San Francisco.

Chapter Twenty

AMONG THE MANY IDIOSYNCRASIES THAT EXISTED within Nette and Zeit's marriage was the notion that Zeit always considered himself to be a Jew. He connected to Judaism deeply, and it seemed—at least to me—that he enjoyed our *simchas* far more than Nette ever did. If I were being snarky, I would posit that Nette didn't enjoy any event at which she was not the center of attention, and she would often go about the business of ensuring that she *was* the center of attention in every room she inhabited. Clearly, her funeral would be no different.

Judaism has very specific and, I think, beautiful rules around funeral rites. It is only in the last thirty years that cremation has been "allowed" (depending upon the sect of Judaism and the family's personal beliefs), but the rites and traditions around how families behave have been quite standard for centuries.

For a start, we bury our dead as quickly as possible, with burial prohibited on the Sabbath and on certain holidays. There were only seventy-two hours between my father's death and his burial. Some families bury within forty-eight hours.

During the funeral, a prescribed set of prayers are offered, including *El Malei Rachamim*, which is a mournful prayer sung for the soul of the departed. When the service ends and the burial is taking place, the attendees protectively make two lines so that the grieving family can leave immediately after they put dirt into the grave, without having to see anything further.

And then the family sits *shiva*, which is a time when the community comes together to pay their respects in the family home, bringing food to comfort the family and making sure their every need is met. *Shiva* traditionally lasts seven days.

The list of customs and traditions is far longer than this, but my point is that it is specific and designed to offer comfort to the family from the moment the loss takes place. And for the most part, it works as the rabbis intended it to work.

Of course, as Judaism was never a core part of Nette's identity, she and Zeit made provisions to be buried at sea in San Francisco. Nette said many times that she didn't believe in things like *shiva* or cemeteries. And so, when I thought about it, a burial at sea made a great deal of sense. They loved travel, and as they aged, travelling by cruise ship became their favorite way to continue to see the world. It made perfect sense that they would want to be scattered on the water that had, in many ways, become a second home to them. And it was just colorful and eccentric enough to inspire conversation, even before they were gone. As ever, they were doing things their way. You can't imagine the looks Nette would get when she boldly proclaimed that she and Zeit planned to be buried at sea. To talk of one's inevitable death during healthy days was shocking enough to people. To choose an avant-garde interment only added to that.

Zeit's final months and the management of his care had become challenging for us when a "family member" had magically appeared. When Zeit came into our family, he told us that he had no family other than ours. He immigrated to America from Taiwan in the 1960s, and during all the years we knew him, we never met a single person from his side. Suspiciously, once he became sick and the estate needed to be managed, a man claiming to be Zeit's nephew appeared. And he was able to provide enough proof for Paula to believe him and grant him a voice in decisions made on Zeit's behalf. To this day, I have never met or spoken with this man. He did not come to meet Paula or visit with Zeit. He never came to court. I was the person there when Zeit and Nette parted for the final time. I was the one with Zeit throughout his final hospital stay, fighting with Paula and the hospital staff because they could not reach this nephew to get his permission for me to visit. And when Zeit died, my mother, sister, and I were the family present to scatter Zeit's ashes on the Pacific. This so-called relative was nowhere to be found.

Being the nice Jewish girl that I am, I had never even imagined what a burial at sea might entail. I really did not consider that there were options other than the traditional ones. But once the clearances (which were complicated and considerable) were given, a date was set, and my mother, sister, and I made the trip to San Francisco.

"What do you think this will be like?" my sister asked. Ever a traditionalist, she found the notion of a burial at sea both fascinating and a bit overwhelming. On some level, we all did.

"I'm not sure," I said, "but in my head, it will be beautiful. And peaceful."

In my head and in my heart, it would be—after many months of no beauty and no peace.

It was a picture-perfect day to be on the water. Warm, sunny, and the waters were calm. In many ways, it was much like Zeit himself, who—no matter what seemed to confront him, including, at times, Nette's abusive energy—was always gentle, soft-spoken, and calm.

Once we boarded the boat, there were the exact beauty and peace to the process and ceremony that I had imagined there would be. The boat held three other families, all in varying states of grief, clutching urns filled with ashes that were to be scattered on the ocean.

The captain took us to a spot just beyond the Golden Gate Bridge and called each family up separately so that there might be a sense of privacy. The farewells were as varied as were the families themselves. Some people prayed. Some sang. Some wept. And then someone from the family would lean over the railing and allow their loved one's ashes to drift away. When it was our turn, as Zeit would have wanted, we said the Mourner's *Kaddish*—one of the traditional Jewish prayers for mourning—and together, we let him go, into the waves and sunshine.

Yitgadal . . . v'yitkadash . . . sh'mei raba . . . Amen.

We whispered it. Ever since my father's death, this prayer always came in a whisper filled with love and sadness and hope that, at last, there might be some peace. Our little ceremony was far more beautiful than I could have possibly anticipated, and even then, knowing that Nette was tucked away in her room in Chicago, I found myself looking forward to the day we would put her to rest in the same manner.

Of course, the day of Nette's sailing was much different. Just as Mother Nature gave us a day that reflected Zeit and his energy, she also gave us a day that reflected Nette and hers.

"*Great*," I quipped. "This weather is just like Nette was. Dark, cold, stormy. *Bitchy*."

My sister, who has never shared or appreciated my at

times irreverent sense of humor, immediately grimaced. "Marra!"

But it was out there. And it was true.

In an homage to Nette and her always impeccable sense of style, I chose to wear Chanel. Flats because we were going to be on a boat but Chanel, nonetheless, and I wrapped my perfectly blown-out hair in an Hermès scarf that I thought Nette might have appreciated. We were both slaves to fashion and the labels that make people think you're quite fancy, so it felt like just the right choice.

"Marra, you look lovely, but I don't think you're going to be warm enough," my mother warned me. "It's so much colder out on the water . . ."

"I will be fine, Mama," I said. "I don't have a coat that goes with this outfit."

I have often pushed against my mother when she tries, as I tell her somewhat affectionately, to micromanage me. And this day was no different. Little did I know that my choice to look just right would come back to haunt me in every way possible.

We set off for Fisherman's Wharf, and the sun continued to hide from us. The wind picked up, and by the time we actually reached the pier, it was cold. Brutally cold. The bone-chilling, teeth-chattering kind that even the best cocoa does not fix.

And for three women from Chicago to be cold says a lot.

"There's a T-shirt shop over there," my sister said. "I'm sure they have sweatshirts or something."

As my sister knows well, if there is one thing that brings out the fashion snob in me, it is seeing families dressed in matching touristy clothing.

"I don't care how cold it is," I said. "I am *not* wearing a tourist fleece. That matches both of you. That we had to buy at Fisherman's Wharf. I just cannot do that."

And yet, my desire not to freeze won out, and there we were. Within minutes, we were dressed in matching fleece jackets stamped with FISHERMAN'S WHARF SAN FRANCISCO—and my perfect Chanel and Hermès funeral gear never saw the light of day. Sadly, the jackets were not nearly enough to insulate us for the dark comedy that lay ahead.

The water was rough. So rough that we were not able to stand without holding on for dear life, and even sitting down required anchoring so as not to slide to and fro on the benches. The captain, the same one from Zeit's funeral, gave instructions far different from the ones issued at Zeit's scattering, given the rough seas.

"I would like to ask that you allow me to scatter the ashes of your loved ones. The inclement weather makes the action much trickier, and if it's not done just right, there is a very good chance the ashes will blow back on you. And we really don't want that to happen."

While I was rarely one to follow instructions, that was all I needed to hear. I happily sat down. "We can say *Kaddish* from here," I proclaimed.

My mother agreed. My sister did not.

"I'll do it. I want to do it," my sister insisted. "Nette would want that."

The captain, my mother, and I tried to talk her out of it for all of the obvious reasons. "There is *no way* this will go well, Alisa," I said. "But if you really want to, I'll be over here. Sitting. *Far* from the water. Like the captain said."

She would not be swayed. I left her to it and took my seat back on the bench with my mother. I'd had enough of Nette's figurative ashes blown back in my face to last me a lifetime while she was living. I did not need any of her actual ashes anywhere near me now that she was dead.

Yitgadal . . . v'yitkadash . . .

We began the *Kaddish* again. My mother and I seated on the bench. My sister leaning over the railing with the urn. Right on cue, the wind kicked up as she began to toss the ashes, and they blew back. All over my sister. And I could not help but laugh. Heartily. And perhaps a bit too loudly to be appropriate.

My sister took it in stride.

"Do *not* say, 'I told you so!' But does anyone have a Handi Wipe?"

That only sent me into deeper laugh-fueled hysteria. I'm

not sure that a Handi Wipe really does the trick when deal-ing with the ashes of a family member, but it was all we had to work with, and so we cleaned her up as best we could and headed back to shore.

We had agreed earlier in the day to go for a nice lunch afterward so that we might have something to look forward to, but as the scattering took less time than we'd anticipated, we had a bit of time between docking and our reservation. So we took a wander on the pier, each of us quietly processing what it meant now that we had laid Nette to rest.

As I stopped to take things in and breathe a bit, one of the many seagulls that had been circling overhead relieved himself—all over me, my Hermès scarf, and my Chanel shoes. I had, of course, removed the horrible tourist fleece the minute the weather allowed me to, so all of my couture was now soiled. And there I was. Covered once again in shit because of Nette.

My sister, now in hysterics of her own, said, "Would *you* like a Handi Wipe?" To me, it was like Nette getting the last laugh—and making sure that she had it her way, even at her own funeral.

I immediately looked at my mother, who was also beside herself with laughter. "*My* lunch," I said, "is going to involve a cocktail, and a strong one at that." And we went off to lunch, all slightly worse for wear but with the job of putting Nette to rest behind us.

I find myself wondering if putting someone to rest really does just that. I have borne witness to the lives and deaths of three people from the closest possible vantage point, and I cannot say that any of them has ever left me, in large ways or in small.

There was no *shiva* after Nette's burial at sea. We simply packed up our bags and returned to Chicago—and to our lives.

Mine forever changed.

Epilogue

AFTER NETTE'S PASSING, IT TOOK SOME TIME FOR the estate to fully settle. And as many months as the settling of the estate took, it took even longer for me to settle—and to process what had taken place over the course of a life lived with these two versions of Nette in it.

My mother inherited virtually everything Nette had. One day, a huge box of jewelry arrived for her. We spread everything out on her bed—all of Nette's truly precious jewels—and took inventory of them. We took guesses as to which pieces came from which of her many, many trips, and we recalled with fondness Nette's great sense of style. It reminded me of Bubbie.

When I was a little girl, it was still a time when most people kept their valuable documents and jewelry in a safe-deposit box in a vault at the bank. My bubbie would often take me with her to the vault where her valuables were stored. And how I loved to go. She would patiently take out all of the jewelry and tell me the history of each piece.

"This ring belonged to my mother. And since you are named for her, one day it will belong to you. She would have loved you." She would set it down and pick up another. "This one your zayde gave me after I found out he had a mistress. Guilt diamonds are always the biggest, it seems. Someday, you can have this one and turn it into something beautiful."

There was so much jewelry in the vault. Each piece was kept in a box that looked like it had history. There were the gorgeous diamond rings, yes. But also necklaces. Men's jewelry, including the diamond rings that my great-grandfather and great-uncles wore. Bubbie kept her memories of her late family members alive through those gems. And every piece told a story—an entire family history told through gold and precious gems.

"These rings are a part of your *yerusha*, mama shayna," my bubbie would say.

Yerusha is the Yiddish word for inheritance. And now it was time to decide what our *yerusha* from Nette would be. Collectively and individually.

The notion of what we inherit from those who came before us has always resonated with me. And while my child brain had created an attachment to inheritance being rooted in *things*, specifically jewelry, Nette's death would teach me that we can inherit far more than simply that which is sparkly and meant to be worn.

My mother gave me carte blanche to choose any of the pieces I wanted for myself. "You choose first," she said. "I will never be able to thank you for what you did for Nette and Zeit. And for me. So let's start here. You choose first."

My mother, ever the most generous person in the world, knew how much I love jewelry.

"Mama, I appreciate it, but there's nothing of Nette's I want," I told her. "Really. If I ever change my mind, I'll let you know. But right now, I don't want anything that belonged to her."

It was a reaction that surprised both of us, for when Nette had first come into our lives, I'd wanted nothing more than for her to someday, in some way, give me a gift of her jewelry. But after all was said and done, I was still processing the whole of my relationship with Nette and what had been a transformative time for me while caring for her at the end of her life. And I no longer wanted any of it.

Even trying on some of the pieces felt uncomfortable to me, almost like they were burning my skin. A bit tight. Not right. And somehow I knew Nette was watching from wherever she was, and she would never have wanted me to have any of her pieces.

My mother and I worked through the collection carefully and selected a set of diamond-and-emerald earrings and a necklace to give to my sister. Much like Nette and my mother, my sister loves jewelry. Even when she is wearing gym shorts and a T-shirt to work in her backyard, Alisa is always bedecked in some form or fashion in something precious. Usually, that includes her wedding band and engagement ring, of course, and a pair of small white-gold-and-diamond hoop earrings I gave her once upon a time. My sister wears diamonds with her nightgown, so the emerald-and-diamond set seemed perfect for her. And, unlike me, having something that once belonged to Nette would bring comfort to my sister.

Then we came across an enormous brass monkey necklace and matching earrings from India. We both sat on the bed staring at them. Never one to shy away from a wry joke, my mother picked up the necklace and held it up to my chest.

"Here. Nette *definitely* would have wanted you to have this."

And we laughed. Harder than we had laughed in quite some time. The hideousness of the necklace combined with the hideousness of the racist use of the word *monkey* to refer to black people was just too good to let go.

For the next couple of years, my mother and I routinely joked about the monkey necklace being my *yerusha* from Nette. For a long time, I left the necklace at my mother's home, tucked away with the dreadful matching earrings in her jewelry drawer. But when I moved to Los Angeles, something inside me decided to take the necklace with me, and I thought it might be a good time to wear it.

It always sparks conversation and, much to my shock, always inspires compliments. I spent the first three decades of my life hiding in plain sight, wanting desperately to be seen by people with loving, admiring eyes and, at the same time, wanting desperately to be invisible so that my family and I might escape from the constant scrutiny and abusive racism.

When I wear the monkey necklace, I *must* be seen. The piece demands it. And so, it turns out that the necklace is part of what has become a perfect inheritance from Nette. The necklace sparked a conversation with someone that led me to write this book, another way I am finally allowing myself to be seen.

Now I think differently about what it means to have an inheritance. Through my experiences with Nette, in her life and in her death, I truly came to understand that there are times when inheriting things from someone who has died can bring great comfort and a sense of connection, and there are other times when the inheritance can bring a sense of disquiet. When it came to Nette, I had had enough disquiet to last many lifetimes.

For me, the inheritance comes through a greater sense of identity. Of who I am. Of what I want to say. Through what I wear. Through the way I speak, on and off the page. Through the way I treat others.

When one is mixed race, it can easily feel like there is a war being waged within. The part of me that has regularly been discriminated against by white people for being brown wants to lash out against white people. The part that has been discriminated against by black people for not being "black enough" or for being Jewish feels the same kind of rage. Layer on top of that being Jewish, and the opportunities to harbor hate, frustration, and anger multiply.

But to hate any of these groups would be to hate a part of myself. And I cannot live that way.

I know far too many people who let the anger—which is absolutely right to own—about living with the constant burn of racism and hate consume them. Holding on to the anger is often not a conscious thing, for public discussions about the nuanced challenges of being mixed race are only just beginning. And until very recently, there has not been a space to talk about it and how it affects us, especially those of us who live at the intersection of race and religion in the way that I do. And we are, as we are with so many cultural discussions, still taking baby steps in many ways.

It is a delicate and often precarious dance to try to find sure-footedness with all of that energy swirling around within. And until the moment I chose to help Nette, I wasn't wholly sure on what ground I really stood. I know now that I stand with two feet solidly planted in love. That both un-consciously and consciously, I choose love. Always. Because of everything I have learned living at this unique intersection of my religious soul and brown skin. Because I know what it is to be deemed unworthy and hated because of my skin color *and* because of my religion. And because I will not be an instrument that puts more hate into the world.

There are two questions I'm often asked when people hear my story.

First, they ask why. Why didn't I just leave Nette in the substandard facility to live out her days miserable and alone? It would have been a just punishment for the person she was and for the way she treated me. For me, the answer is simple and straightforward.

Perhaps there is some truth to the notion that Nette deserved to die unattended and in squalor, but to have knowingly allowed that to happen is not who I am. I now know that I don't choose to be vengeful, even when it might be justified. I can be a creature fueled by love but not be held prisoner by it. I can be loving even to someone who is not loving in return. That is certainly as beautiful a gift as any piece of jewelry I might buy. It is more beautiful.

I have come to find that racists—and people who struggle to see that we are, all of us, beautiful in our identities—are often unhappy. And on some level, they lash out, wanting us to join them in that space. My time with Nette taught me well that I do not need to allow anyone to dictate my identity—or to steal my joy. Or my sense of compassion. Or my ability to love.

The other question is far less simple for me to answer. People ask if I loved Nette. While I acted out of love, I cannot answer that question, even to this day. I suppose that, as a child, I loved her as a child loves: with a simple heart and no questions. She was my great-aunt, and so I loved her because she was family. When I grew old enough to understand that she not only did not return any sort of love, obligatory or otherwise, but also hated me on a few fronts, I was so filled with pain, sadness, and anger that there wasn't much room left for love.

In the end, when Alzheimer's stripped Nette of who she was and she became a being who loved me as I once had her, with the heart of a child, it is fair to say we were both transformed.

I do not know who I might be today had I chosen the other path when we got the phone call saying Nette was in trouble, had I made my decision from a place of pain, anger, revenge, or even hate. I don't really want to know.

I only know who I am because of the choice I did make. That to live and act from a place of love is what is right for me.

And for me, that is enough.

Acknowledgments

To have written this book is a dream I didn't know I had. So, too, is to now share my heartfelt thanks with the very special people who made it possible.

I will never be able to express my gratitude to my mother for giving me life and for encouraging me to be free to express myself in ways she was never able to herself. For her love, her generosity, her support, I have no words. How I love you, Mom.

To my late father, who is with me always, I am forever grateful. I carry his heart in every moment of my life.

To my siblings, Alisa and Merrill, I am grateful. For our differences. For our similarities. For your love. Your understanding. Your support. For our laughter and our tears. I love you deeply and always. And to your families, who made our family grow—Keith, Giaden, Geneve, Lindsey, and Addisyn—I am profoundly grateful and filled with love.

To my friends who are my family—Tracy, Rosa, Tom, and Rob—who held my hand, told me that I can and must, made me laugh, and cheered me on as I stripped away my every defense, I love you and am so grateful to have you in my life.

To Josh, Lisa, and Kira, who so generously lent their eyes, hearts, and wonderful support, I am grateful from the bottom of my heart.

To every friend and stranger who has reached out with a voice of support, I am touched beyond words and thankful.

To my agent, the truly lovely and brilliant Murray Weiss, I send my thanks for believing that my voice and experience should be put on the page.

To my smart, soulful, and insightful editor, Jessica Easto, I send deepest thanks for being my partner on one of the most profound and terrifying journeys of my life. And to Doug Seibold and the Agate team, for seeing something special in my story.

And . . . to Nette. In spite of everything.